To Megan and Stephen
JVB

In memory of my mother
JLP

To Diane
TMR

Biographies

Jeffery V. Bailey, CFA, is director, Financial Benefits & Analysis at Target Corporation, where he supervises the investment programs and administration of the company's defined-benefit and defined-contribution plans, nonqualified retirement plans, and health and welfare plans. Formerly, Mr. Bailey was a managing partner of Richards & Tierney, a Chicago-based pension consulting firm specializing in quantitative risk control techniques. Prior to that position, he was assistant executive director of the Minnesota State Board of Investment, which manages the pension assets of Minnesota public employees. Mr. Bailey has published numerous articles about pension management. He co-authored the textbooks *Investments* and *Fundamentals of Investments* with William F. Sharpe and Gordon J. Alexander and co-authored the Research Foundation of CFA Institute publication *Controlling Misfit Risk in Multiple-Manager Investment Programs* with David E. Tierney. Mr. Bailey received a BA in economics from Oakland University and an MA in economics and MBA in finance from the University of Minnesota.

Jesse L. Phillips, CFA, as a member of the Treasurer's Office of the University of California system, is responsible for risk management for the system's more than $60 billion of pension, endowment, defined-contribution, and working capital assets. His duties include asset allocation, investment policy development, and the integration of risk management into all aspects of the Treasurer's investment process. Prior to joining the Treasurer's Office, he worked at Northrop Grumman Corporation—first, as senior corporate mergers and acquisitions analyst and later, as manager of risk analysis and research in the Treasury Department. Mr. Phillips also worked as corporate planning analyst with Florida Power & Light Company and as senior financial analyst with Storer Communications, both in Miami, Florida. He began his career as an accountant/analyst at BDO Seidman and was a licensed CPA. Mr. Phillips earned his BA in mathematics and economics and MA in applied mathematics at the University of California, Los Angeles, and his MBA in finance at the University of Miami.

Thomas M. Richards, CFA, currently serves as a consultant to the Nuveen HydePark Group. He is co-founder of Richards & Tierney, an investment consulting firm that provided specialized investment analytical services to large investment institutions. In 2007, Nuveen Investments acquired Richards & Tierney. Mr. Richards has published a variety of articles in pension finance literature and has been a frequent speaker at investment conferences and seminars. He is a co-author with Jeffery V. Bailey and David E. Tierney of the chapter on performance evaluation published in the textbooks *Managing Investment Portfolios* and *Investment Performance Measurement.* He earned a BS in mathematics from Bucknell University and an MS in finance (with distinction) from the Pennsylvania State University. Mr. Richards is chairman of the board of trustees for the Research Foundation of CFA Institute.

Acknowledgements

Attempting to place yourself in the position of a new trustee, particularly one without an extensive investment background, is not an easy task. Once you've become familiar with the role and the subject matter, it is difficult to recreate the concerns and questions that arise when someone is initially joining an investment committee. Thus, a major challenge in writing this book was to present the "newcomer" perspective and provide fledgling trustees with sufficient information to operate effectively but not overwhelm them with facts and concepts. In searching for that balance, we benefited from the comments of numerous individuals who provided valuable reviews of the book during its development. The authors would like to thank Gary Brinson, Beth Dubberley, Bruce Duncan, John Freeman, Doug Gorence, Joyce Keller, Scott Kennedy, Ed Kunzman, John Mulligan, John Nagorniak, Ann Posey, Bob Seng, Larry Siegel, and Dave Tierney for their assistance and support. We also acknowledge financial support from the Research Foundation of CFA Institute.

Contents

Foreword.   xi

Introduction   1
   Our Target Audience   1
   Organization of the Book   3
   Takeaways.   9

Session 1. Governance Structure   10
   Governance Basics.   10
   Roles and Responsibilities   11
   Lines of Authority.   15
   Accountability Standards   18
   More on the Trustees   19
   Takeaways.   20
   Questions Molly Should Ask.   21

Session 2. Investment Policy.   23
   The Importance of Investment Policy   23
   Defining Investment Policy   23
   Policy Asset Mix: Selection and Rebalancing   25
   Investment Policy as a Stabilizer   26
   Reviewing Investment Policy   27
   The Investment Policy Statement   28
   Takeaways.   29
   Questions Molly Should Ask.   30

Session 3. The Fund's Mission   32
   The Fundamental Conflict   33
   Liabilities   36
   Contributions   37
   Takeaways.   39
   Questions Molly Should Ask.   39

Session 4. Investment Objectives.   41
   Criteria for Effective Investment Objectives   41
   Examples of Investment Objectives.   44
   Takeaways.   46
   Questions Molly Should Ask.   46

Session 5. Investment Risk Tolerance   47
   Return Is Only Half the Story   47
   Types of Investment Risk   48
   Measuring Risk   49
   Relationship between Risk and Expected Return.   51

Managing Risk through Diversification 51
Risk Budgeting. 53
Investment Risk Tolerance. 53
Takeaways 55
Questions Molly Should Ask 55

Session 6. Investment Assets 57
Types of Investment Assets 57
Diversifying across Asset Classes 57
Market Indices 58
External and Internal Investment Management 59
Active and Passive Management 62
Separate Accounts and Commingled Funds. 63
Alternative Investments. 64
Takeaways 66
Questions Molly Should Ask 67

Session 7. Performance Evaluation. 69
The Importance of Performance Evaluation 69
Performance Measurement. 70
Performance Benchmarks 72
Performance Attribution. 73
Performance Appraisal 75
Putting It All Together. 77
Takeaways 78
Questions Molly Should Ask 79

Session 8. Ethics in Investing. 81
Recognized Principles of Trustee Ethical Conduct. 81
"Shades of Gray": Recognizing and Resolving Ethical Dilemmas. 82
Establishing Ethical Conduct Guidelines. 82
Takeaways 84
Questions Molly Should Ask 84

Appendix A. Freedonia University Endowment Fund Governance Policy
Statement. 85

Appendix B. Freedonia University Pension Fund Investment Policy
Statement. 87

Glossary of Investment Terms. 97

Further Reading. 105

Foreword

For more than 35 years, I have had a strong commitment to the Research Foundation of CFA Institute. The Foundation strives to facilitate in-depth, high-quality discussion of investment issues oriented to the practical application of investment finance. The research covers all fields of investment and is directed at all parties who play a role in investment decision making. The body of work that the Research Foundation has produced is an invaluable library for anyone who is directly or indirectly involved with investment asset management.

A Primer for Investment Trustees ("*Primer*") is a powerful text, in keeping with the Research Foundation's mission. The authors provide a comprehensive discussion of investment issues relevant to a very important constituency of the investment community—namely, investment trustees. Most of these individuals have had successful careers but not necessarily in the investment field. In their capacities as trustees, they are not responsible for day-to-day decision making at the funds that they serve, but they do bear responsibility for setting investment policy and assessing performance. They serve at public and private pension funds, endowments, foundations, insurance companies, Taft–Hartley funds, and a wide variety of special-purpose trust funds. What these funds have in common is a reliance on their trustees to provide policy direction and oversight of their investment programs.

Although trustees do not need to be investment experts, they must have a solid grasp of basic investment principles in order to exercise good judgment in their investment decisions. In my many years of investment experience, I have worked with a wide array of investment trustees and I have seen how a lack of investment understanding can seriously harm an investment program and limit the likelihood of achieving the fund's mission.

Gaining a proper understanding of investment principles can be a challenging experience for trustees, particularly new trustees. They often receive only a rudimentary orientation session and must learn by listening to what is said by others, experts and nonexperts alike—who are often difficult to tell apart. There are few resources to which trustees can turn for help. In my judgment, the *Primer* is an ideal resource for filling that void and providing trustees with a knowledge base that will enable them to fulfill their responsibilities successfully. Authors Jeff Bailey, Jesse Phillips, and Tom Richards provide an excellent focus from the perspective of the trustee while avoiding the use of complex investment terminology. The *Primer* is an "easy read," which is particularly helpful to trustees who likely have other full-time jobs.

Although the *Primer*'s main audience is investment trustees, it also can be beneficial to investment professionals and other parties who work directly or indirectly with investment trustees. For example, the fund's staff, outside consultants, professional investment managers, actuaries, accountants, custodians, lawyers, fund contributors, and fund beneficiaries interact with fund trustees. All these groups can benefit by understanding the investment trustee's perspective, circumstances, and responsibilities. Such an understanding will facilitate better communications and allow all parties to work together more effectively.

I wholeheartedly recommend the *Primer* to all investment trustees—new and experienced—to investment professionals who work with trustees, and to those who have an interest in understanding the role and responsibilities of an important constituency of the investment community.

Gary P. Brinson, CFA
Chicago, Illinois
October 2010

Introduction

> As the old saying goes, what wise men
> do in the beginning, fools do in the end.
>
> —*Warren Buffett*

Let's face it. Few business assignments are more intimidating than being placed in a position of responsibility outside your area of expertise. Surrounded by subject matter experts awaiting your direction, you find yourself actually expected to make decisions. Even though you are told in the beginning that there are no dumb questions, you don't want to provide the exception to the rule. A multitude of technical reports full of unfamiliar and complex concepts are quickly thrown at you. Your real day job keeps you busy and offers few opportunities for learning about your new position. So, you sit silent at meetings, lacking confidence, frustrated and concerned about your ability to contribute productively. Well, welcome to the world of the newly appointed investment trustee.

Our Target Audience

Over the years, we have been fortunate to work with trustees coming from many walks of life. Often, these individuals, although quite successful in their respective professions, possess little investment knowledge or experience. Yet, they take on responsibility for the oversight of financial assets that have a material impact on the welfare of their funds' beneficiaries. If you count yourself as one of these diligent laypeople, then you belong to the target audience for this book.

From the start, we want to put your mind at ease on one critical point: Extensive investment expertise is not required for you to serve effectively in a trustee role. Nevertheless, for you to exercise good judgment in making decisions, you should possess at least a working understanding of basic investment principles and concepts. We believe that you can acquire this knowledge with a modicum of effort. The purpose of this book is to provide trustees, particularly if they are new to their positions, with a primer that will help them begin to successfully fulfill their responsibilities.

Throughout the book, we use the term "trustee" broadly (and not in the legal sense of the word) to describe any person serving on a governing body who is charged with high-level supervision of investment assets. This governing body could be a pension investment committee at a corporation, an investment advisory council at a public retirement system, a board of trustees at an endowment fund, or something similar. If you are a member of such a group, then for our purposes, you are an investment trustee, regardless of your particular title. Importantly, we recognize that you do not have day-to-day responsibility for *managing* investment portfolios. Instead, you periodically receive reports from and meet with the staff of the fund that you oversee to discuss broad issues related to investment policy and performance results. As a result, the challenges and opportunities that you face are quite different from those of the staff who must manage ongoing operations.

Our audience also extends to the investment professionals who directly interact with you and to other parties who have a special interest in your fund. These persons include the fund's staff, outside consultants, professional investment managers, actuaries, accountants, custodians, lawyers, and importantly, the beneficiaries of the fund. In most cases, the topics that we cover are familiar to investment professionals. Other interested parties may have little or no such knowledge. Nevertheless, both groups can benefit by taking your perspective and considering the learning curve and questions that you face, thereby gaining useful insights into how to work with you effectively.

Although many of the standard issues in investment finance have quantitative aspects, we avoid the use of formulas in this book and, instead, describe the relevant issues in a conceptual, straightforward manner (which, in many cases, is a harder task than presenting mathematical relationships). Our discussion will proceed as though we are having a conversation with a new trustee who has just become a member of a fund's investment committee. We will refer interchangeably to the "trustees" and the "investment committee."

The new trustee could be a representative of a company's human resources department who has been appointed to the retirement fund investment committee. She could be a retired judge who has been asked to serve as an investment trustee for a special asbestosis trust fund. He could be a college alumnus who started a successful technology company, earned a vast sum of money (a considerable amount of which he donated to his alma mater), and now serves on the board of directors of the school's endowment fund. She could be a union shop steward who has been chosen to serve on the investment committee of a *Taft–Hartley fund*. Or he could be a former professional wrestler who, as governor of a major state, has the responsibility of chairing the investment board of a multi-billion-dollar public pension fund. (Note the type of fund in the previous sentence that is in boldface italics. As part of your learning process, we provide at the end of this book a Glossary of Investment Terms. Beginning with Session 1, terms that are defined in the glossary are shown in the text the first time in boldface italics.)

We have had personal experience over the years with each of these types of individuals and many more. All of the trustees with whom we have worked earnestly desired to do a good job during their "watch." Just as you do, they wanted the fund to be in as sound or even better shape when they left the investment committee as it was when they joined it. Of course, this outcome often depends on the performance of the capital markets, something over which you have no control. Nevertheless, favorable investment markets have a way of masking uninformed and poor trustee oversight, and weak investment markets often expose deficiencies and magnify a trustee's *fiduciary* risk. Our objective is to help you understand important investment issues and ensure that appropriate policies, processes, procedures, philosophies, and people are in place so that the fund may succeed regardless of the investment environment.

Organization of the Book

In this book, we focus on subjects critical to your success as a trustee. We believe that to create and maintain a well-managed investment program, you and your fellow trustees should have, at a minimum, a solid grasp of the following foundational topics as they apply to your fund: governance structure, investment policy, the fund's mission, investment objectives, investment risk tolerance, investment assets, performance evaluation, and ethics in investing.

We have divided this book into sessions dealing with each of these topics. In each session, we present the material in the form of an overview that an investment staff person for the fund is providing to a new trustee—Molly Grove. Molly started a very successful company providing high-tech information services to medical doctors in small communities. Because of her success and philanthropy, she is held in high regard and has been named a regent of the state's university system. As part of her responsibilities as a regent, she has been assigned to serve on the university's investment committee. The investments of the university system include a defined-benefit (DB) plan, a defined-contribution (DC) plan, an endowment fund, a foundation, and a self-insurance trust. The investment committee has oversight responsibility for all of these funds. We refer to Molly and the rest of the investment committee as dealing with "the Fund." For the most part, the Fund may be any of the university's investment pools because the trustee's role usually is not materially different among the specific types of funds involved. On those occasions when we need to make a distinction regarding one fund or another, we specifically point out which fund is being discussed.

Our conversation with Molly on each of the topics is followed by a recap, called "takeaways." We then offer a set of questions we believe would be useful for Molly to ask the staff member with whom she is having the conversation.

Although these lists are not exhaustive, they do provide you with an opportunity to drill down further into each session topic. New trustees are often uncomfortable asking questions of experienced investment staff. We want to assure you not only that the example questions that we provide (and others, of course) are appropriate to ask but also that the staff members may not necessarily have ready answers. Thus, both parties can learn through intelligent questions.

You might wonder about one topic conspicuously lacking in this book—namely, legal issues relating to fiduciary responsibilities of the trustee. We have excluded such a discussion not because the associated issues are unimportant but because we are investment practitioners, not attorneys. The material concerning legal responsibilities is complex and voluminous. Also, there are substantial differences in fiduciary law, unlike in investment issues, among the various types of funds and geographical boundaries. As a result, the topic deserves its own publication written by a legal expert.

In spite of this disclaimer, we will go out on a limb and mention one basic legal principle that we believe you should understand. (Please discuss this principle with your plan's legal counsel if you want to know more.) That principle is termed the "prudent investor rule." The core of this rule is as follows:

> A trustee shall invest and manage trust assets as a prudent investor would, by considering the purposes, terms, distribution requirements, and other circumstances of the trust. In satisfying this standard, the trustee shall exercise reasonable care, skill, and caution. (Uniform Prudent Investors Act 1994)

Although many of the matters requiring investment expertise can and should be delegated to experts, *you* must have a solid grasp of the "purposes, terms, distribution requirements, and other circumstances of the trust." We believe that this book will provide you with valuable assistance toward this end.

Before we begin the discussion between Molly and the investment staff, let's first conduct a brief summary of the topics that we will cover.

Governance Structure. Governance structure encompasses the responsibilities of the various types of decision makers within an investment program and how these decision makers relate to one another. In addition to you and the other trustees, decision makers include such groups as the investment staff, consultants, investment managers, custodians, and actuaries.

You will find that a solid governance structure effectively addresses three key areas: responsibility, authority, and accountability. Numerous questions flow from an examination of the governance structure, including the following: What functions are required to successfully run an investment program? What is their importance to the investment program? Who typically performs these functions? What sorts of reporting relationships exist among the decision makers? What are the incentive arrangements? Where does the buck stop?

Within the governance framework, you, as a trustee, are positioned at the top. Trustee responsibilities may vary considerably from fund to fund. In part, these differences relate to the size and resources of the fund. Nevertheless, how you carry out your responsibilities does affect investment program performance. Trustee approaches can range from an unhealthy involvement in the smallest operational decisions to a similarly unproductive disengaged attitude. In our discussion, we will consider what your oversight responsibilities should entail, which decisions you should be responsible for, and which ones you should delegate. We believe the *process* by which you arrive at decisions is, in many ways, as important as the actual decisions. In particular, you should take ownership of your oversight responsibilities. You should delegate to those who have the required expertise, experience, and authority to do their jobs. And you should hold all parties accountable for actions that they take (or fail to take). We believe this basic philosophy distinguishes strong governance structures from weak ones.

Investment Policy. Your most valuable contribution as a trustee will be setting investment policy for the fund. Although you don't manage the fund on a day-to-day basis, you do determine the key strategic priorities for the fund that are encompassed in the investment policy. Others may assist you in drafting that policy, but only the trustees can establish it as the roadmap for the fund.

In broad terms, investment policy defines how the investment program will be managed. Investment policy specifies the procedures, guidelines, and constraints for decision making and management. Ideally, you will thoroughly document those decisions in a written investment policy statement.

Your focus in setting investment policy should be on how you trade off expected return and risk in seeking to achieve the fund's objectives—essentially, the creation of a risk budget. In establishing this trade-off, you will be required to specify how the fund should be allocated to various types of assets and, within each of those types, what sorts of investment strategies should be used and what benchmarks the investment results will be assessed against.

You will find that investment policy serves its most useful role as a stabilizer in stressful markets. In good times, pressure rarely builds to change the investment program. Not so when the storm clouds roll in. People have a natural tendency to predict the worst will happen when times are bad and, conversely, to extrapolate that good times will last forever. The ability to stick to your established strategic priorities in periods when the temptation to alter the investment program is most intense will save you from counterproductive changes at just the wrong time.

The Fund's Mission. Among the key elements of investment policy is establishing the mission of the fund. A fund is a pool of assets created to accomplish certain society-enhancing goals. Simple as the task may sound, your first important job as a new trustee is to understand the fund's purpose. In a broad sense, all funds exist to provide payments to beneficiaries. For example, corporations and public entities establish defined-benefit or defined-contribution plans to provide retirement benefits to employees. Civic-minded persons contribute to endowment funds to grant long-term financial support to worthwhile causes. Insurance companies establish investment funds to pay future loss claims. Parents set up education trusts to fund their children's future schooling.

In simple terms, regardless of what type of fund you are working with, three things happen: (1) money—that is, contributions in various forms—flows into the fund from external sources, (2) the value of the fund increases or decreases depending on how the investment markets perform and how the fund's assets are invested and managed, and (3) money flows out of the fund to pay the fund beneficiaries—that is, benefit payments in various forms are made. There are differences among funds with regard to the amount and certainty of the inflows and outflows, but you should understand how, why, and when money is expected to flow into and out of the investment fund.

A fund typically has numerous stakeholders, and their needs and desires often conflict with one another. Thus, a fundamental responsibility of a trustee is to articulate and prioritize these conflicting aspects of the fund's mission.

Investment Objectives. Investment policy outlines the path that you wish your investment program to follow. As part of setting that direction, you need to express how you, as a trustee, define success for the program—that is, its objectives. You should specify what sorts of investment outcomes signal that the investment program has been successful. To avoid confusion and second guessing, you will want these investment objectives to possess certain characteristics. Specifically, they should be clear and objective, measurable, attainable, reflective of the trustees' willingness to bear risk, and specified in advance of the evaluation period.

Investment objectives play both a prospective and retrospective role. Prospectively, they help you structure your investment program in terms of the rewards that you expect and the risks that you are willing to take in order to meet the fund's mission. Retrospectively, they assist you in assessing the effectiveness of the investment program and thereby suggest when to take corrective action and when to continue with current practices.

Investment Risk Tolerance. Many trustees focus solely on investment returns earned by their funds without taking the time to understand the investment risk involved in producing those returns. By "risk," we mean the potential for serious losses in pursuit of the fund's mission. The myopia regarding risk occurs because returns are visible but risk is not. Yet, you have little control over the returns earned by the fund. Instead, your responsibility is to engage with the other trustees to establish the investment committee's collective risk tolerance.

The staff and consultants will assist you in expressing this risk tolerance. They should also present you with procedures for measuring and controlling the amount of risk the fund is assuming. The process of setting this risk budget can be formal and quantitative, or it can be subjective and qualitative. The key is that you recognize that higher expected returns come at the price of increased risk. Furthermore, taking more risk does not guarantee higher returns; it only makes such returns *possible*. You should periodically review reports that indicate whether the risk-budgeting procedures are being followed and whether the fund's risk management efforts are effective.

You will need to differentiate between your views about the appropriate risk level for your own investment portfolio and the appropriate risk level the investment committee should take as it invests the fund's assets. Your personal financial circumstances and investment time horizon will not be the same as those of the fund that you oversee. As a trustee, you must be able to set aside your personal opinions and consider only what is best for the investment program over the long run.

Investment Assets. You will want to be familiar with how different assets are categorized and managed. For investment policy purposes, fund decision makers divide the investment world into various asset types, called "asset classes." Typical asset class designations include equities, fixed income, real estate, and so on. The granularity of the categorizations varies widely among funds.

The grouping of investments into classes is supported by the availability of a broad array of market indices representing publicly traded equity, fixed income, and other types of securities divided into seemingly uncountable variations. These indices serve the valuable functions of defining the *opportunity set* for the investment program and providing a window on the risk and return history of specific asset classes. That history, in turn, becomes an important input for developing allocations to the various asset classes.

Regardless of the types of assets held, you will need to make decisions regarding the broad structural aspects of how the investment program is managed. You have the choice of assigning staff members to manage directly all or a portion of the fund's assets (internal management) or using outside investment firms (external management). Each type of management offers certain advantages and disadvantages, although external management tends to be the prevailing model.

Another important issue involves whether to manage the fund's asset class investments passively or actively. You can choose either to seek to match the performance of a given index (passive management) or to attempt to exceed the performance of that index (active management). The higher expected returns of active management must be weighed against the associated additional risk and incremental cost.

In addition to the traditional investments in publicly traded stocks and bonds, funds often hold positions in various forms of illiquid assets, which are referred to as "alternative investments." These assets include, to name a few, real estate, venture capital, and hedge funds. Although these investments are more complex and expensive to manage than the traditional kind, funds use them in the hope of earning a premium return by bearing the associated illiquidity risk and taking advantage of the opportunity to search among potentially less efficiently priced assets.

Performance Evaluation. Performance evaluation provides a regular assessment of the fund's performance relative to your investment objectives. Properly conducted, performance evaluation reinforces the hierarchy of accountability, responsibility, and authority defined in the fund's governance structure. Performance evaluation serves as a feedback-and-control mechanism by identifying the investment program's strengths and weaknesses.

Performance evaluation can be broken down into three primary components:

- *Performance measurement*—calculation of the returns earned by the fund and comparison of those returns with the returns of appropriate benchmarks.
- *Performance attribution*—identification of the factors that led to the fund's performance relative to the benchmarks.
- *Performance appraisal*—assessment of the sustainability of the fund's returns relative to those of the benchmarks.

Trustees sometimes confuse performance measurement with performance evaluation. But simply measuring returns is only the beginning of the evaluation process. By asking what caused the performance of the fund relative to that of appropriate benchmarks and by inquiring into the quality (i.e., magnitude and consistency) of that *relative performance*, you gain valuable insights into the effectiveness of the investment program.

Ethics in Investing. Trustees, along with all of the other parties involved in the fund's governance structure, should always be conscious of the question, Is this [action being contemplated] in the best interests of the fund's beneficiaries? Unfortunately, the answer is not always obvious. Certain actions can be construed to profit a particular party other than the fund's beneficiaries. A fine line often exists, which calls for carefully exercised discretion.

Our discussion of ethical investment practices is meant to create awareness of the subject's importance. You don't need an exhaustive list of "dos and don'ts." Rather, your emphasis should be on the importance of the policies and procedures designed to be most advantageous to the fund's beneficiaries. You should ensure that the fund has management controls that incentivize ethical investment behavior—not only of the trustees and investment staff but also of all parties involved in the fund's governance structure. These guidelines should be consistent with industry best practices.

Takeaways

- We use the term "trustee" to broadly refer to any person serving on a governing body charged with high-level supervision of invested assets.
- Extensive investment experience is not required to serve effectively as a trustee.
- A working knowledge of basic investment principles and concepts, however, will help you exercise good judgment in making decisions in your trustee role.
- This book is divided into chapters dealing with the following foundational topics: governance structure, investment policy, the fund's mission, investment objectives, investment risk management, investment assets, performance evaluation, and ethics in investing.

Session 1. Governance Structure

> Knowing others is wisdom; knowing the self is enlightenment.
> Mastering others requires force; mastering the self needs strength.
>
> —*Lao Tzu*

Welcome, Molly, to the Freedonia University *Investment Committee*. We have a lot of material to cover with you in this orientation. We will stick to the basics and avoid going into too much detail on any particular topic. You will have plenty of opportunities outside of this meeting to discuss the ideas that we cover today.

Governance Basics

Molly, let's begin our discussion of your role as an investment trustee by considering how the Fund's decision makers interact with one another. Many persons and organizations make investment-related decisions at various levels for the Fund. The framework that connects these decision makers is the *governance structure*. A strong, well-articulated governance structure provides the mechanism for decision makers to function together effectively. A weak, ill-defined governance structure breeds confusion and acrimony.

Nothing can guarantee that the Fund won't experience disappointing investment outcomes. A strong governance structure is your best assurance, however, that if such a result does occur, it won't have been caused by preventable weaknesses inadvertently designed into the investment program.

Because the *trustees* sit at the apex of the Fund's organizational hierarchy, familiarity with your role and with that of others in the governance structure is essential. Moreover, if you can satisfy yourself that the governance structure is sound, then you will rest easier knowing that you have fulfilled an important *fiduciary duty* to the Fund.

We like to think of the Fund's governance structure as a three-legged stool. Each leg of the stool provides support and balance for the investment program. And like a stool, the investment program cannot stand without all three of these legs. The three legs of the Fund's governance structure are as follows:

- *Roles and responsibilities*—a delineation of functions that the various decision makers are assigned to perform.

- *Lines of authority*—a description of the latitude that decision makers have to carry out their responsibilities and a specification of their reporting arrangements.

- *Accountability standards*—a statement of expectations regarding the effectiveness of the decision makers combined with a set of procedures for reviewing and, if needed, responding to the actions of those decision makers to whom responsibility is delegated.

There are other aspects of the Fund's governance structure that keep it strong:

- *Due diligence*—appropriate oversight of the investment program's operations.
- *Checks and balances*—decentralized decision making and the ability of one set of decision makers to challenge others.
- *Reporting and monitoring*—adequate and timely distribution of information to decision makers.
- *Transparency*—access to the details behind the Fund's investment transactions, fees, expenses, and cash flows.
- *Compliance with industry best practices*—periodic review of other funds' operations and modification of the investment program when appropriate.

The investment committee articulates the Fund's governance structure in a formal policy document called the "governance policy statement" (GPS). In particular, Molly, you will use the Fund's GPS to delineate the roles and responsibilities of the trustees and the *staff*. The clarity this document provides helps all decision makers avoid misperceptions and confusion. It promotes an open dialogue among the Fund's decision makers and permits them to concentrate on their specific assignments. The investment committee bears responsibility for periodically reviewing and, as appropriate, updating the GPS. As an example, **Appendix A** in your materials contains a copy of the Freedonia University Endowment Fund's GPS. Unfortunately, most funds do not clearly document their governance structures. Instead, they base their structures on a set of organizational precedents and practices, some of which have been written down and some of which simply follow tradition. For funds in this situation, it is important that regular discussions take place among the decision makers to ensure that they understand and remain in agreement regarding the governance structure's key features.

Roles and Responsibilities

Five primary groups of decision makers have a significant impact on the investment program: you and your fellow trustees, the investment staff, investment management firms (who we will refer to as "*investment managers*"), the *custodian bank*, and the *investment consultant*(s). Other persons and organizations, such as legal and accounting groups, affect the design and function of the investment program to a much smaller degree. We generally won't consider them as we review the governance structure. So, let's first introduce the principal parties and briefly describe their roles within the investment program.

Trustees. As we mentioned, the trustees reside at the pinnacle of the investment organizational pyramid. The buck, so to speak, stops with the Freedonia University Investment Committee. In essence, you and the other trustees are responsible for the overall success of the investment program. However, because you have no hands-on involvement in implementing the Fund's investments, you fulfill your responsibility by determining an appropriate direction for the investment program, by empowering experienced people to carry the Fund in that direction, and finally, by monitoring and evaluating investment results.

Specifically, the trustees hold the responsibility for setting broad *investment policy* and overseeing its implementation. (We will discuss investment policy in Session 2.) You carry out that responsibility in three primary ways. First, the trustees appoint the chief investment officer (CIO), and he reports directly to you. On an annual basis, the investment committee conducts a formal review of his job performance, the results of which determine his compensation for the following year. You share that review with the CIO in a frank discussion behind closed doors. You also approve his selection of senior staff members and sign off on his evaluation of those staff members. This leadership team is critical to effectively translating your vision of investment policy into a concrete investment program.

Second, the trustees work with the CIO to develop and, on occasion, update the *investment policy statement,* which describes the key aspects of the Fund's investment policy. Typically, the staff initiates these updates, but in the end, the investment committee alone decides whether to alter the investment policy.

Finally, the investment committee periodically reviews investment results as presented by the CIO and determines whether the Fund is on course to achieve its objectives as envisioned in the investment policy. If the trustees believe that the Fund is performing appropriately, then you act to reinforce the positive aspects of the organization and encourage corrections of any weaknesses. If significant changes are warranted—a rare occurrence—then you can step in and make key senior staffing and policy changes to maintain the integrity of the investment program.

Before leaving the discussion of trustees, we would be remiss if we did not mention an issue that complicates governance in many funds. It is the fact that governance is often divided between two or more groups of trustees. For example, there may be an investment committee to make investment decisions, a finance committee to determine the level of spending or the structure of *benefits,* and a funding committee responsible for the level of *contributions* that flow into the fund. Without clear communication and cooperation among these committees, promises to spend or pay benefits may be incompatible with the investment environment or risk-bearing capacity of a fund or they may be inconsistent with a fund's expected cash flows.

Investment Staff. The investment staff carries out the day-to-day operations of the investment program. Led by the CIO, the staff converts the investment policy established by the trustees into specific implementation procedures, such as keeping the Fund's allocation to designated *asset classes* and investment managers at assigned target levels. The staff maintains appropriate *liquidity* to meet the Fund's obligations; performs oversight of the Fund's investment managers, both individually and in aggregate; and makes modifications to the investment manager lineup as deemed necessary. The Freedonia trustees have delegated the authority to hire and fire investment managers to the CIO, although at some other funds, the trustees retain that discretion. The staff has responsibility for maintaining bank custodial relationships and also for periodically preparing reports for the investment committee and other interested parties regarding the activities and performance of the investment program. The managers regularly report their investment results to the staff; they offer explanations for those results and discuss current strategies. As part of the due diligence process, the staff typically meets with the managers at least once a year to discuss their current investment strategies and investment performance results. The staff periodically visits the managers' offices to gain a greater awareness of the managers' operations and personnel.

Although it is not the case with most organizations, at some funds, the staff directly invests some or all of a fund's assets. If the organization is large enough and has the ability to pay sufficient compensation to attract talented people, this approach can be cost-effective. Such in-house investment management presents its own unique governance issues, however, because risk-control responsibilities become intertwined with incentives to maximize returns. That arrangement puts added responsibility on the trustees to actively monitor the decision making and *risk management* of the investment staff. For that reason alone, many funds choose not to manage assets in-house. We'll return to external and internal management in Session 6 on investment assets.

The size of the investment staff differs widely among organizations. Generally, funds with more assets can afford to, and do, hire larger staffs than funds with fewer assets. Funds that manage assets internally carry even larger staffs. Smaller funds may have only one or two professionals on the staff, and the trustees may even carry out certain staff roles to compensate for this lack of people.

Some funds, particularly small ones, outsource all their staff functions. Certain external providers offer a full package of services, such as investment management, fund accounting, *performance evaluation*, brokerage, payment of benefits, and actuarial reports. The organizations that offer these services include money managers, bank custodians, investment consultants, actuarial firms, and investment brokerage companies. Although outsourcing is an attractive option for some funds, this arrangement can limit a fund's investment options and does not eliminate a trustee's fiduciary liability. Moreover, it can create *agency conflicts* between the provider and the fund because of different incentives. (For example, a service provider may seek to maximize its fee revenue rather than focusing on offering value to the fund's beneficiaries.)

The attraction of outsourcing is largely economic. Hiring and retaining a competent investment organization is expensive. The size of Freedonia University's invested assets justifies hiring a CIO and staff. Nevertheless, small funds and those with limited financial resources to hire staff members should carefully weigh the costs and benefits of outsourcing.

Investment Managers. Investment managers, whether represented by external organizations or by internal staff, make decisions regarding which particular assets to buy and sell. The staff members at most funds prefer to hire a variety of managers, largely organized around various types of *financial assets*, such as U.S. and non-U.S. equities, *fixed-income securities*, and *private equity*. Some "absolute return" (or *hedge fund*) managers operate under broader *mandates* and may choose among various asset types in search of attractive returns.

The investment committee at Freedonia University has directed the staff to use *active management* as opposed to *passive management*. The active managers use their investment analysis and portfolio management skills to attempt to outperform, after fees and expenses, *benchmarks* consistent with their areas of expertise. Passive managers, in contrast, attempt to match the performance, before fees and expenses, of their benchmarks. Although active managers bring with them the opportunity to exceed the return of their benchmarks, they also carry with them the risk of underperformance. This *active management risk*, combined with the higher management fees and transaction costs associated with active management, has led trustees at some funds to manage part or all of their assets passively. We'll talk more about active and passive management in Session 6 on investment assets.

Within their designated investment mandates, the Fund's active managers have broad discretion to construct portfolios. The staff develops, and the investment committee approves, investment guidelines that specify the types of *securities* that will be held in the managers' portfolios, the level of risk that the managers are expected to take, and the benchmarks with which their investment results will be compared. In some cases, the managers' compensation is based on their performance relative to their benchmarks. Well-constructed investment guidelines place enough restrictions on the managers' investment activities to prevent large negative performance "surprises"—those in which results fall far from expectations. Still, well-designed guidelines should not seriously constrain the managers' exercise of their investment judgment.

Custodian Bank. The Fund's custodian bank supplies important safe-keeping, recordkeeping, and valuation services. For many of the Fund's invest-ment managers, the bank holds ownership of the publicly traded securities in which the managers invest. The bank carries out settlements of trades ordered by the managers (but not the trades themselves). Periodically, the bank reports details of the Fund's recent transactions and current holdings. The valuation of those holdings can be a trivial task in the case of public equities but can be problematic with esoteric assets, such as complex fixed-income securities that rarely trade. The Fund's custodian bank also offers ancillary services, including securities lending and *performance measurement*. It also provides the raw material for the various audits the Fund undergoes annually. With the requirements in recent years for greater financial-reporting transparency, the custodian bank has taken on broader reporting responsibilities.

Consultants. The investment committee retains investment consultants to provide a variety of services. These consultants offer an extension of resources and expertise that would be too costly to maintain full time. Funds differ in their use of consultants. Some rely heavily on them, whereas others use them for narrow and specific purposes. Many organizations use consultants for two primary tasks: to advise on strategic issues, such as investment policy, and to provide manager selection and performance evaluation. In the case of strategic issues, consultants provide independent information and opinions to the trustees.

Consultants do not serve as a parallel staff but, rather, complement the staff's work. In the case of manager selection and performance evaluation, consultants have specialized resources, skills, and experience that are difficult for an investment staff to acquire and maintain. As requested, consultants regularly attend investment committee meetings to offer their insights. Some of the trustees meet regularly with the consultants, just as the CIO and other senior staff members do, to seek advice on issues facing the Fund.

Lines of Authority

Molly, as you well know from your own professional experiences, responsibility and authority must go hand in hand. To give certain decision makers the responsibility for performing aspects of managing investments but not to provide those same decision makers with the authority to carry out their professional judgments is a sure means of creating a dysfunctional organization. Investments, with their highly quantifiable results, are exceedingly prone to various forms of second guessing that undermine official delegation of authority.

Unfortunately, this problem most commonly occurs in the relationship between the trustees and the investment staff. Explicit authority may be delegated by the trustees to the staff, while some or all of the trustees retain *implicit* authority. The Freedonia investment staff has been fortunate to maintain a positive working relationship with the investment committee. For example, the trustees authorize the staff to retain and dismiss investment managers, a common arrangement at many funds. The trustees have been careful in the past not to second-guess staff decisions concerning manager retention. At some other funds, the trustees constantly ask probing questions about the individual investments undertaken by the managers and then pass judgment on the results of those investments. In many of those instances, the clear intent is not simply to understand how those managers are operating but to suggest that the staff's decisions in hiring those managers were not appropriate.

The implied message in such a situation is that, despite the explicit hiring authority granted to the investment staff, the trustees retain the authority to hire and fire managers. The staff then interprets this message as a warning not to act too independently of the trustees. The staff may fire some managers whom its members approve but judge to be in disfavor with the trustees, or the staff members may fail to hire an attractive manager out of concern that the trustees may not approve of that manager. But the trustees at these funds generally do not possess the expertise to identify successful managers prospectively, and in the end, the implicit withholding of authority from their staff corrodes the manager selection process. The trustees may ultimately be correct about a particular manager, but unless they can suggest fundamental deficiencies in their staff's *processes*, their after-the-fact criticism of the processes' results can disempower and demoralize the staff. The Freedonia University Investment Committee wisely avoids this problem by focusing its evaluations on the performance of the Fund's aggregate assets as opposed to the individual managers' investment results.

Of course, a similar problem can exist between the investment staff and investment managers. Managers are explicitly delegated authority to make portfolio construction decisions for their clients' accounts within specified investment guidelines. Again, the staff can implicitly withhold that authority by frequently questioning portfolio decisions after the fact. However, because investment managers are more diversified in their client bases than a fund staff, the managers are better positioned to fend off these efforts on the part of the staff than the staff is prepared to hold the line against meddling trustees. Nevertheless, if a staff constantly picks away at individual decisions on the part of a fund's managers, the managers may withhold their more unconventional ideas from the portfolios, to the ultimate detriment of the fund.

The solution to these problems is conceptually simple but, at times, difficult to put into practice. It is that (1) the lines of authority must be clearly specified and (2) the supervising decision makers must scrupulously refrain from reaching down to the reporting decision makers and attempting to control decisions. Furthermore, the reporting decision makers need to feel empowered to push back and remind the supervising decision makers in those instances when the line between explicit and implicit authority becomes blurred. Documenting the lines of authority through the GPS is the ideal solution, but even if such documentation exists, a culture of full and frank discussions must be maintained.

Like most organizations, the investment committee has authorized an organizational chart that identifies the Fund's lines of authority. We have attached that chart to your presentation materials as **Figure 1**. In addition to simply specifying the lines of authority, the investment committee has incorporated the other elements of a strong governance structure mentioned earlier—due diligence, checks and balances, reporting and monitoring, transparency, and compliance with best practices—to align implicit with explicit authority.

Figure 1. Freedonia University Investment Committee Organization Chart

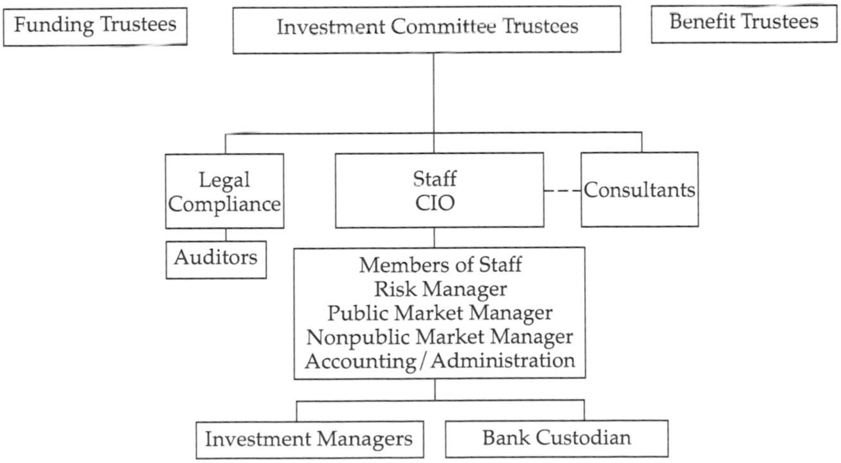

Accountability Standards

Accountability provides the third leg of a strong governance structure. You can assign responsibility for an investment function to a person or a group and give that person or group the authority to carry out that function. Those steps are necessary—but not sufficient. Everyone wants responsibility and authority; few, however, want accountability. Yet, if the appropriate level of accountability is missing, then the trustees cannot expect that person or group to be properly incentivized to carry out the function in a way that best meets the goals of the Fund.

As a result, the investment committee has mandated that accountability standards be established throughout the governance structure. Wherever key decisions are being made, the trustees have insisted that accountability standards be set for the decision makers. Regardless of their specific design, those accountability standards have common characteristics. They are

- appropriate and realistic (i.e., commensurate with the given authority),
- established in advance,
- agreed to by both the supervising and subordinate persons or groups,
- evaluated in the context of the expected range of outcomes, and
- designed to provide formal procedures for supervising authorities to review the results of subordinates' decisions.

Consider that the investment committee assigns the CIO a set of accountability standards for use in his annual evaluation. Those standards include both a "personal results" component and an "investment results" component. The personal results component relates primarily to how well the CIO interacts with the staff and trustees. Topping this list must be open and direct communication. For example, an appropriate expectation, Molly, is that you and the other trustees be comfortable asking the CIO any question that comes to mind and that you receive a prompt and understandable answer. Timely reporting, effective management of the staff, and productive relationships with other stakeholders and outside organizations will also factor into this personal evaluation.

The investment results component is based on the Fund's management relative to defined expectations. The CIO cannot guarantee investment outcomes, and his investment performance objectives recognize that fact. Still, you should want the CIO to feel that if the Fund performs well, he will participate in that success. For example, the trustees have decided that the Fund's return relative to established benchmarks and the maintenance of the asset mix within policy guidelines should factor into the CIO's investment results component.

In an investment program, surprises will always occur, some of them potentially quite disappointing. Often, it is not clear how to evaluate them, even with a solid set of accountability standards in place. Among other questions, you will likely want to ask whether the CIO had the authority to make a different outcome happen and whether the process under which the adverse outcome occurred was prudent and properly implemented. In addition, you should consider whether the bad result could reasonably have been predicted and prepared for. Molly, your conclusions will likely involve a fair amount of subjectivity. One of the primary reasons you were invited to be a trustee, however, is that you have a history of good judgment. In an uncertain investment world, that characteristic is of critical importance.

More on the Trustees

Your fellow trustees recognize that appropriate organizational design of the investment committee can enhance the Fund's governance structure. As a result, the trustees have focused on several key aspects of membership and meeting format, including the following:

- number of members,
- member selection,
- diversity of experience,
- member tenure,
- leadership,
- frequency of meetings,
- meeting length, and
- meeting agendas.

The Freedonia University Investment Committee is composed of seven trustees. Having too many trustees makes scheduling meetings difficult; having too few trustees increases the potential for one or two persons to dominate the decision making. A subcommittee of the Board of Regents takes nominations and ultimately recommends trustees to the full board for approval. This independent selection process prevents current trustees from controlling the choice of new members. As a result, new trustees join without owing an allegiance to existing committee members.

In recruiting attractive trustee candidates, the regents look for individuals with a wide range of career experiences. Although the regents consider investment knowledge to be a positive attribute, they certainly don't view it as a prerequisite to be selected as a trustee. In fact, several trustees have been chosen because of their experience in areas outside of investing—managing large businesses, for example. The regents prefer to strike a balance on the investment committee between investment experience and other backgrounds. A diverse membership makes it less likely that "groupthink" will dominate the board's decisions regarding investment policy. Because of their diversity, the trustees are an active group who vigorously debate the relevant issues and are open to dissenting, but constructive, ideas.

The trustees serve three-year terms and can be reappointed for one additional term before they must leave the investment committee for at least two years. In this way, the trustees do not become too comfortable in their positions but have enough time to understand the university's funds and to function effectively. Moreover, this forced turnover periodically brings in fresh ideas through new members. Terms are staggered to avoid wholesale membership change and a resulting loss of institutional knowledge. The investment committee's chair and vice chair are appointed by the regents—again, to prevent one individual from holding too much power within the group.

The investment committee members hold in-person meetings at least three times a year and arrange for telephone meetings as necessary. The in-person meetings are important because they promote effective discussion among the trustees and between the trustees and the investment staff. The trustees prefer quarterly meetings to keep on top of pressing issues and to review investment results on a timely basis. The CIO, in consultation with the investment committee chair, controls the meeting agenda. The trustees favor meetings that last no more than half a day, thereby allowing the participants to remain fresh and productive throughout the meeting.

Funds take varying approaches toward membership and meetings, but the investment committee at Freedonia is fairly conventional. Institutional situations cause some differences (for example, a public pension plan may have statutory membership requirements). Other differences may be the result of decisions made long ago that the funds have grown accustomed to. Regardless, the trustees review the membership and meeting guidelines periodically to stay in line with best practices.

Takeaways

- The governance structure is the framework that connects a fund's various decision makers to one another.
- The key elements of the governance structure are described in a formal governance policy statement (GPS).
- A sound governance structure has three primary components: roles and responsibilities, lines of authority, and accountability standards.
- Roles and responsibilities define the functions the various decision makers are assigned to perform.

- Lines of authority both describe the power given to decision makers to carry out their responsibilities and specify to whom those decision makers report.
- Accountability standards state the expectations regarding the effectiveness of the decision makers and the procedures for reviewing their actions.
- Sound governance also requires
  - appropriate diligence procedures,
  - checks and balances with regard to the various decision makers,
  - timely reporting and monitoring,
  - transparency of decisions and details of investment transactions and holdings, and
  - compliance with industry best practices.
- Important trustee membership issues include the number of trustees, selection process, diversity of experience, tenure, and leadership.
- Meeting schedules also deserve consideration, including meeting frequency, meeting length, and meeting agendas.

QUESTIONS MOLLY SHOULD ASK

About governance policy

- Is the Fund's governance structure formally documented? If so, may I see the document? If a GPS does not exist, how is the Fund's governance structure understood and communicated?
- How is the governance of the Fund organized? Who are the key participants in the structure? How do they relate to one another in terms of accountability and authority?
- Are responsibility, accountability, and authority appropriately aligned in all areas of the Fund's governance structure? Are there any areas of concern? If so, what are the issues involved?

The investment staff

- How is the staff organized? What are the professional backgrounds of the CIO and his senior managers?
- How is the CIO evaluated? What have been the recent results of his evaluations?
- Does the staff have the resources to adequately carry out its responsibilities? If not, what are the concerns?
- What is the compensation structure (e.g., base salary, bonus, deferred compensation, perquisites) for the CIO? Who determines staff compensation?
- How is the staff budget determined? What is the size of that budget? How is it allocated by major account?

- What investment management decisions are delegated solely to our CIO and the staff? Do we have a set of performance expectations for these persons with respect to those decisions?

Relationships among key decision makers

- What investment management decisions does the investment committee retain in whole or in part? What is the purpose of retaining these decision-making responsibilities?
- What regular reports do the staff, the custodian, and the consultant provide to the investment committee?
- Are the trustees relatively involved as a group in terms of managing the staff, or do they tend to be "hands-off"?
- When there are disagreements between the trustees and the staff, how are they resolved? Are there any issues that continue to fester?
- Where are the Fund's assets held? Who has authority to access those assets? What types of safeguards do we have to prevent unauthorized access to the Fund's assets?
- What valuation methods does the custodian use to value the assets? What sorts of quality checks are applied to the reported numbers?
- Do we retain a consultant? If so, how do the trustees and the staff use our consultant? What is our record of following the consultant's recommendations?
- How long has it been since the consultant and the custodian relationships were reviewed? What were the results of those reviews?

The trustees

- Who are the current trustees? How long have they been on the investment committee? What are their backgrounds?
- Who selects the trustees? What is the selection process? What criteria are considered most important in selecting a new trustee?
- What types of training are provided to new trustees?
- How is the leadership of the trustees chosen? Are there informal leaders who differ from the officially chosen leaders?
- How are the trustee meetings usually run? What topics tend to dominate the agendas? Is there a bias toward reviewing past performance as opposed to addressing forward-looking strategic issues?
- Are the minutes of the past trustee meetings available for review?
- How do the trustees protect against groupthink?
- What are the core beliefs of the trustees as a body?
- How are the trustees evaluated, both individually and as a group?

Session 2. Investment Policy

> Once the "what" is decided, the "how" always follows. We must not make
> the "how" an excuse for not facing and accepting the "what."
>
> —*Pearl S. Buck*

Virtually all well-run investment programs are built on the foundation of a
thoughtful investment policy. Molly, in our discussions, we should be clear that
the most important function that you and the other trustees perform is establishing and maintaining the Fund's investment policy.

The Importance of Investment Policy

Why is investment policy so important? If the trustees can't develop and convey
a clear sense of what the Fund is attempting to achieve and how they expect
staff members to go about accomplishing those objectives, then the investment
program will be directionless and the trustees and staff will be prone to pursue
ineffective approaches that lead to unsatisfactory results. Yogi Berra's succinct
wisdom aptly applies to investing: "If you don't know where you're going, you're
liable to end up somewhere else."

Some funds fail to adopt sound investment policies. Others adopt sound
investment policies but fail to follow them diligently. In either case, the funds
typically rely on *ad hoc* approaches to investment management. The manifes-
tations of these inadequate investment practices include a short-term focus
(often on issues of secondary importance, such as the hiring and firing of
managers) and inattention to important long-run issues. These behaviors
generate a hodgepodge of frequently changing and inconsistent investment
strategies. *Ad hoc* management also hinders trustees in conducting realistic
appraisals of their objectives and keeps them from implementing stable,
productive investment programs that achieve their objectives.

Defining Investment Policy

We should clearly define what is meant by the term "investment policy." The
investment committee thinks of its investment policy as a combination of
philosophy and planning. It expresses the trustees' collective attitudes toward
important investment management issues: Why does the Fund exist? How does
the investment committee define success? To what extent are the trustees
willing to accept the possibility of large losses? How do the trustees evaluate
the performance of the investment program?

The investment committee also considers the investment policy to be a form of long-range strategic planning because it delineates the trustees' specific investment goals and how they expect those goals to be realized.

Essentially, any relatively permanent set of procedures that guides the management of a fund's assets can be deemed to be the fund's investment policy. Nevertheless, a comprehensive investment policy will address many of the issues that we are covering in our discussions, including

- the fund's mission,
- *investment risk* tolerance (i.e., the ability and willingness of the trustees to bear investment risk),
- investment objectives,
- the *policy asset mix*,
- investment management structure, and
- performance evaluation.

Different financial circumstances and attitudes toward seeking returns and bearing risk cause funds to adopt different investment policies. There is nothing wrong with that. Simply put, there is no "correct" investment policy. However, an effective policy tailors the issues we just identified to a fund's specific circumstances, whether that fund is a corporate pension plan, a public pension plan, an endowment, or a family office.

The investment committee often speaks of the Fund's investment policy as the "rule book" for the investment program. Despite the fact that there is no single solution to the challenge of investment policy design, the "rules" for all types of funds appropriately contain many of the same essential elements. That is because an investment program can be successful over the long run only if it operates under a well-defined plan, and success can be evaluated only in light of clearly stated investment objectives. An investment policy that incorporates the fundamental elements that we cover provides the necessary planning framework. That may sound like common sense, or rather good business practice, and it is. And like any sound business practice, it should be universally applicable to the Fund's investment program, regardless of how the composition of the staff or the investment committee changes over time.

Investment policy identifies the key roles and responsibilities related to the management of the Fund's assets. Not only does the investment policy establish accountability, but it also helps to minimize conflicting interests. For example, the university's defined-benefit pension plan exists to provide retirement income to *plan participants* but is partially paid for by the state's taxpayers (or shareholders in the case of a private plan). The trustees may feel accountable to taxpayers in some way, even though they are supposed to be loyal solely to the plan participants. Similarly, the investment staff cares about the participants but also thinks about job protection and maybe earning a bonus. External investment managers worry about their businesses and their fees while, at the same time, being responsible to participants. Although no set of rules can eliminate these conflicts, a sound investment policy can contribute to a solution by stating clear accountabilities and enhancing the transparency of an investment program.

Policy Asset Mix: Selection and Rebalancing

A central part of a fund's investment policy is to choose asset classes and investment strategies within those asset classes that, in aggregate, produce a well-diversified portfolio. To begin, the trustees need a workable understanding of the underlying risk and *expected return* characteristics of these asset classes. (We will discuss the term "asset class" more thoroughly in Session 6 on investment assets; for now, think of asset classes as broad categories, such as *stocks*, *bonds*, and *real estate*.) From that understanding, the investment committee can determine the desired allocation to each asset class so that, in total, the investments reasonably can be expected to produce the required return over the long run with an acceptable level of *volatility* in results. This process is referred to as "setting the policy asset mix," and it directly relates to the level of investment risk considered appropriate for the Fund by the trustees. (We will discuss how the investment committee determines the appropriate level of risk in Session 5 on investment risk tolerance.) The investment committee approves the policy asset mix as a list of asset classes, a target percentage allocation for each, and a range around that target allocation within which the actual allocation may fluctuate before *rebalancing* back to the target is required. As an example, you can review the policy asset mix of the Freedonia University defined-benefit pension plan in **Appendix B**, which we have provided in your materials. Again, we will have more to say on the particular asset classes in the policy asset mix during Session 6 on investment assets.

Obviously, nothing in life or business is perfectly obvious all of the time. Nor will any set of rules, however robust, always point to the most profitable course of action. The investment committee does not expect its policy asset mix to generate the desired returns year in and year out. Rather, the trustees' approach is that when others are greedy and bidding up the price of certain asset classes and the expected return on those asset classes decreases, the trustees are willing to take a little less risk by selling off some of those appreciated asset classes if their allocation has moved above the top of the approved range. Conversely, over the course of a *market cycle*, when markets plunge and investors are fearful, certain asset classes tend to be shunned. These asset classes then become cheaper and thus have higher expected returns. At those times, the investment committee is willing to take on more risk and buy those asset classes if their allocation has moved below the approved range. This process is called "rebalancing back to the policy asset mix." Because the trustees, staff, and consultants are all human, the Fund's investment policy seeks to overcome cognitive biases that cause decision makers to fear and avoid these rebalancing opportunities just at the time when they offer the Fund the greatest potential returns.

Investment policy helps manage risk by starting with a clear statement of the mission and objectives of the Fund, identifying the key risks faced by the Fund, assigning accountability for those risks, setting up metrics for determining success, and then defining procedures for evaluation, oversight, and management of the Fund. Molly, as a trustee, you cannot be expected always to make correct investment decisions, but you are always expected to carefully consider the relevant risks and how they should be managed before making a decision.

Investment Policy as a Stabilizer

The investment committee established the Fund's investment policy independent of current market conditions. Although the trustees allow for discretion on the part of the staff and the investment managers to take advantage of attractive near-term market valuations, the trustees, in setting the investment policy, have accepted as given the long-run opportunities afforded by the capital markets and the Fund's obligations to its beneficiaries. A consistently applied investment policy produces successful results not because of any unique investment insights but because of its concentration on the Fund's primary goals and the continuity of its investment strategies.

Investment policy would be of little significance if it were merely a perfunctory description of the investment program. Instead, it derives its importance from the complex and dynamic environment that the trustees confront in setting a direction for the Fund. The trustees and staff need a logical and consistent framework within which to make decisions.

The Fund's investment policy is an "autopilot" setting for normal times and a stabilizer for the investment program during stressful markets. The Fund's investment policy needs to be flexible, but in the past, the trustees have made changes only during periods when fundamental conditions changed significantly, either externally or internally. The investment committee has always maintained that the threshold for conditions to qualify as "significant changes in conditions" should be quite high. If not, the urge to change policy in response to short-run market conditions can be overwhelming. Following this urge will, in turn, defeat one of the key virtues of investment policy—namely, to keep decision makers from acting rashly, from succumbing to either greed or, particularly, fear.

That last point bears repeating. Trustees sometimes fail to appreciate that adherence to the investment policy will produce its greatest benefits during periods of adverse market conditions. At these times, the temptation builds to alter a sound investment program as the fear of even worse future calamities increases. Decisions to change course in these situations inevitably prove costly. The investment committee has been fortunate to avoid those outcomes. The existence of a well-thought-out investment policy has forced the Fund's decision makers to pause and consider why the existing policy was established in the first place and whether the current adverse market conditions were actually predictable—not in their timing but in their intensity and (paradoxically) their unexpectedness. That type of review has made it possible for cooler heads and a longer-term outlook to prevail on the investment committee. It has allowed the trustees to stay with their long-term policy during market downturns and avoid locking in current losses while eliminating the possibility of recovering those losses as markets reverse.

Reviewing Investment Policy

As we discussed, investment policy is not immutable. The investment committee periodically reviews—and, on occasion, modifies—the Fund's investment policy. Think of a business plan, Molly. When would you change your company's strategic plan? Certainly if the basic structure of competition were to change (such as when key suppliers gain pricing power or a shift occurs in the customer base), disruptive technologies appear, or big changes occur in government regulation—any of these circumstances would call for a review and possible modification of your business plan.

You and the other trustees might find it appropriate to alter the Fund's investment policy if the Fund's obligations were to change materially. If changes in the investment landscape, such as new practices or products, were to occur, then you also might want to alter the policy to ensure that potential opportunities are not missed. If the investment committee truly were to conclude that the long-run expected risk–reward relationships among asset classes had fundamentally changed, that change too might warrant a modification in investment policy. (That conclusion is, of course, quite different from merely observing that particular asset classes have recently performed poorly or well relative to one another.) Nevertheless, the investment policy rarely requires alteration simply because the factors that could justify a change in the investment policy are themselves not generally prone to near-term transformations.

Regular discussions of the investment policy aimed at educating the Fund's decision makers serve a productive purpose. They reinforce the logic of the current policy and thereby reduce the chances of unnecessary alterations.

Conversely, reviews directed toward the constant reassessment of existing policy are counterproductive. Frequent investment policy changes take on the tone of active management, thus blurring the distinction between policy and operations, to the detriment of the investment program.

If the trustees believe that a change in investment policy is warranted, then you should recognize that the modifications are almost never time sensitive and should not be hurried. In fact, the greater the seeming urgency of proposed policy changes, the more likely that those changes are really active management decisions posing as policy issues.

The Investment Policy Statement

The investment committee has formalized the Fund's investment policy in a written document called the "investment policy statement" (IPS). An IPS summarizes a fund's key investment policy decisions and explains the rationale for each decision. The level of detail in an IPS will vary among investment organizations. Some organizations may prefer to provide more information than others, particularly those with more complex investment programs. Nevertheless, an IPS serves the same role for all funds: It enforces logical, disciplined investment decision making, and it limits the temptation to make counterproductive changes to an investment program during periods of market stress. (Recall that Appendix B is a copy of the Freedonia University defined-benefit pension fund's IPS for your inspection.)

The Fund's IPS is not a set of broad statements such as, "Look both ways before you invest." Rather, it contains an explicit recipe for the investment program stated in terms of minimum and maximum allocations to various asset classes, levels of allowable risk, and so forth. The IPS also contains guidelines for investing within an asset class. Those guidelines may be stated as a list of requirements or prohibitions or in terms of a budget for various types of investment risk. Another key element is the establishment of performance objectives for the Fund and for individual asset classes. These objectives provide a reference point for evaluating the success of the Fund's investment strategies.

The IPS serves three primary functions:

- It facilitates internal and external communication of investment policy.
- It ensures continuity of policy during periods of turnover among the Fund's trustees and staff.
- It provides a baseline against which to evaluate proposed policy changes.

Regarding the first function, the IPS communicates the Fund's investment policy to insiders (the trustees and staff) and interested outsiders (for example, the Fund's investment managers or its beneficiaries). The IPS helps prevent confusion over interpretation of the Fund's investment policy. A regular presentation of the IPS keeps investment policy fresh in the minds of the Fund's decision makers. For that reason, the investment staff includes the Fund's IPS in the set of materials for every investment committee meeting.

Regarding the second function, the IPS serves as a permanent record that enhances continuity in the investment program. Turnover among the trustees and top staff members is inevitable. For newcomers, the IPS provides a concise and accessible reference. Its existence also makes clear that the policy is a product of a thorough and deliberate process; thus, the IPS reduces the urge on the part of new decision makers to impulsively propose revisions to the pension fund's existing investment policy. For that reason, Molly, as part of your orientation, you should take the time to carefully review the IPS of each of the Freedonia University funds and ask questions about the contents.

Finally, the IPS serves as a standard against which to consider proposed changes to the Fund's current investment policy. Any such potential changes can be directly compared with existing policy, making the merits of the changes easier to evaluate and limiting the chances that emotional appeals for change will sway decision makers. Over the years, the existence of the Fund's IPS has prevented a number of potentially ill-advised alterations to the investment strategy.

Only the trustees can establish investment policy for the Fund. You and the other trustees are the ultimate fiduciaries, and it is your responsibility to provide the investment philosophy and long-term direction for the Fund. True, in many organizations, the investment policies are drafted by the investment staff, sometimes with the aid of a consultant. But in the end, the trustees have the responsibility, authority, and ultimate accountability for the Fund's investment policy. If the trustees are ever sued for losing money, a properly crafted IPS—and documentation that the policy has been scrupulously followed—is a strong defense.

Takeaways

- The most important functions that the trustees perform are to establish and maintain the fund's investment policy.
- Investment policy is a combination of philosophy and planning.
- Investment policy expresses the trustees' attitudes toward important investment management issues.
- Investment policy is a form of long-range strategic planning that delineates the trustees' specific investment goals and how the trustees expect those goals to be realized.
- A comprehensive investment policy addresses
  - the fund's mission,
  - *risk tolerance*,

- investment objectives,
- the policy asset mix and rebalancing policy, and
- performance evaluation.

- Investment policy acts as a stabilizer for the investment program and thereby helps avoid costly shifts during unusual market conditions.
- Investment policy is changeable, but the case for modifications should be held to a high standard and should be based on truly fundamental changes, not simply transitory movements in market conditions.
- Central to investment policy is the policy asset mix—the long-run desired allocation of a fund to designated asset classes.
- The investment policy statement (IPS) formalizes investment policy in a written document, summarizing a fund's key policy decisions and explaining the rationale for those decisions.
- The IPS serves three primary functions:
  - to facilitate communication of investment policy,
  - to ensure continuity of policy during periods of trustee and staff turnover, and
  - to provide a baseline against which to evaluate proposed policy changes.

QUESTIONS MOLLY SHOULD ASK

- Do we have a formal written IPS? If not, why not? If so, may I have a copy to review?
- Does our IPS discuss the underlying rationale for the policies that we have adopted?
- Is our IPS broadly disseminated to key stakeholders?
- What duties do I have as a trustee under our investment policy?
- As a group, do the trustees understand our investment policy well? Is the investment policy thoroughly covered in new trustees' orientations?
- What are the key factors that could cause us to rethink and revise our investment policy?
- Of the primary components of the investment policy, which ones have the broadest agreement among the trustees? Which ones have the most divided opinions?
- Are there investment policy changes that the staff has proposed but the trustees have opposed? If so, what is the background behind those desired changes?
- When was the Fund's investment policy changed materially, and why was it changed?

- Do we have a record of the changes that have been made to our investment policy with a description of what, when, and why we made the changes?

- When was the current version of our investment policy adopted? Who wrote the current version of our investment policy? Who reviewed this version? Our legal counsel? Our consultant? Did they make substantive comments, and if so, what were they?

- Is there a regular review of the investment policy? Who takes the lead in those discussions—the trustees or the staff?

- If our investment policy is considered to be the rule book for running our investment program, would you say that our rules are comprehensive and prescriptive in design or loose and advisory?

- What is the policy asset mix of the Fund? What was the process by which it was determined?

- What rebalancing rules does the staff follow to ensure that the Fund's actual *asset allocation* is in line with the policy asset mix?

- Are those rebalancing rules implemented without question or does the staff have discretion when and how to implement them?

- Are there legal restrictions that govern the investments of the Fund over which the trustees have no discretion?

- Can you cite instances in which our investment policy has actually acted as a stabilizer in periods of distressed financial climates?

Session 3. The Fund's Mission

> Choose always the way that seems best, however rough
> it may be; custom will soon render it easy and agreeable.
>
> —*Pythagoras*

Molly, as a trustee serving on the university's investment committee, you have oversight responsibility for the assets of the *defined-benefit (DB) pension plan*, the *defined-contribution (DC) pension plan*, the *endowment*, the *foundation*, and the self-insurance trust. Broadly speaking, each fund has an investment mission, which is to provide financial benefits to certain parties. Also, a common feature of these funds is that they invest in pools of assets that were contributed from particular sources for particular purposes. The differences among the funds consist of the timing and certainty of the benefits that flow out of the investment pool, the contributions that flow into it, and the specific uses to which the benefits will be put.

To help you understand the concept of a fund's mission, we decided to focus on the Freedonia University DB pension fund. We based this choice on the fact that the investment policies of DB pension funds, in general, involve interesting and diverse missions. Also, a legally binding commitment exists to pay pension benefits at specific times and in specific amounts.

The DB pension plan that the university provides to its employees is quite similar to your own company's plan, Molly. A notable difference, however, is that the state's taxpayers stand behind the university's pension promise whereas it is your company's stockholders (and, ultimately, the U.S. taxpayers through the Pension Benefit Guaranty Corporation) who guarantee your company's benefit obligations.

With respect to the university foundation and endowment funds that you also oversee as a trustee, note that contributions to them vary over time and that the withdrawals or benefits typically are based on a percentage of the funds' value. However, you should appreciate, in particular, that the endowment fund makes a material contribution to the university's operating budget and that an unwritten rule exists that the possibility of a decline in the amount of money the endowment provides should be minimized.

As for the DC pension plan that the university offers to employees, you do not have any direct responsibilities relating to the actual allocation of assets. Rather, the trustees have a responsibility to provide employees with a variety of investment options (primarily *mutual funds* and similar types of investment vehicles) that allow employees to create and manage their retirement assets in a manner consistent with their needs and circumstances.

With that background, let's begin our discussion of the DB pension fund.

The Fundamental Conflict

So, exactly what is the mission of the university's DB pension fund? At first, the answer to that question might seem obvious. However, on further reflection, Molly, you may find that it is much more complicated.

At the most basic level, of course, the Fund exists to ensure the availability of sufficient assets to pay the pension benefits promised to the plan participants. (The term "participants" refers not only to current employees and retirees but also to former employees whose benefits are vested.) There would be no reason to maintain the pool of assets if these obligations did not exist. The importance of securing the benefit promise is so great that current tax law allows taxable private-sector plan sponsors to deduct contributions that are made to their funds and exempts income earned by their funds from taxation. For a tax-exempt not-for-profit entity such as Freedonia University, U.S. law requires that the Fund serve solely the interest of the plan beneficiaries. Because the university places assets in the Fund, it backs its promise to pay pension benefits with more than simply its good faith. Plan participants can rely on the assets held in the Fund if the university should ever become insolvent.

The Fund's mission is far more complex, however, than this simple directive would imply. The university (and, by implication, the investment committee) has other important stakeholders in the Fund in addition to the plan participants. At the top of the list are the state's taxpayers (in the private sector, shareholders). Despite the overriding importance of securing the pension promise, decision makers and stakeholders should never forget that a financially healthy organization is required for pension benefits to be offered. If the Fund's mission doesn't take into account the financial needs of the university, then the plan may eventually be neglected, poorly funded, or possibly even terminated. None of these outcomes would serve the interests of plan participants.

The university generally prefers to contribute as little money to the Fund as possible without diminishing its ability to pay benefits. The cost of providing pension benefits equals the present value of all contributions made over the DB pension plan's life. The university wants the investment committee to minimize that cost. Private-sector plan sponsors also want to keep contributions as low as possible. They often have an additional objective in that they desire to minimize the volatility of the accounting expense associated with operating their pension plans.

You can imagine situations in which other groups view themselves as stakeholders in the fund, including labor unions, state and federal legislatures, social activists, and so on. Although these groups may not have a direct impact on the Fund's core mission, the university and investment committee have not neglected their concerns.

Given the complexity of the Fund's mission, it is not surprising that various aspects of that mission come into conflict. The primary conflict is between the intent to assure the security of the promised benefits and the desire to minimize the present value of plan contributions made over the long run. Plan participants want benefit security, but they have to realize that the university has many pressing expenditures and must keep pension costs down. Conversely, the university wants pension costs to be as low as possible, but it must recognize the value that the DB pension plan provides for attracting and retaining a productive and motivated workforce.

By far the most direct means of securing the benefits promised to plan participants is to maintain a well-funded plan. The ratio of plan assets (i.e., the value of the Fund) to plan liabilities is called the *"funded ratio"* (also called the *"benefit security ratio"*). A plan that has more assets than liabilities is considered to be *overfunded*, and one that has fewer assets than liabilities is *underfunded*. The higher the funded ratio, the greater the protection offered to plan participants. The greater the extent to which the ratio exceeds 100 percent (full funding), the more cushion the trustees have to protect against shocks to the value of assets or liabilities eating into benefit security.

Now, if the investment committee were *solely* concerned with benefit security, the trustees would place the Fund in low-volatility investments. That would likely entail holding much of the Fund in high-quality bonds with interest rate and inflation sensitivity similar to that of the plan's liabilities. If that were the case, the university and the plan participants could be highly certain that there would always be assets of sufficient amount to pay all benefits. The funded ratio would fluctuate little over time.

The problem with that approach is that it is likely to result in considerably higher contributions. There is a simple rule that expresses the essence of the situation:

Benefit payments = Contributions + Earnings on contributions.

The source of benefit payments is simply whatever the university puts into the Fund plus any earnings that can be generated on those contributions. If you assume for the moment that the benefit payments are fixed, then the higher the returns that the Fund earns, the lower the required contributions the university has to make, and vice versa. Just as importantly, if the university wants to increase benefit payments in the future, then either the university must make more contributions or the Fund must earn higher returns—or some combination of the two must occur.

In general, the university prefers to minimize contributions over the long run, which frees up financial resources that can be put to other productive purposes. To keep the university's contributions to the pension fund as low as possible, the investment committee creates an investment portfolio with relatively high expected returns. So, in addition to bonds, the trustees have chosen to invest in higher returning assets, such as *common stocks*. But the returns on those stock investments tend to be volatile. That volatility will tend to cause the level of fund assets to fluctuate in the short run, making the funded ratio less stable than if the Fund invested only in bonds. The result will be more instances in which the university will have to make a contribution to offset unexpected declines in the funded ratio. (For private-sector plan sponsors holding stocks in their funds, the pension expense reported in the accounting statements will also be less predictable.)

So, even though the investment committee recognizes that the primary aspect of the Fund's mission is to ensure benefit security, the committee still faces a conflict between secondary aspects of the Fund's mission: *Avoiding volatility in contributions and the funded ratio* versus *keeping the costs of funding benefits low*. How do the trustees go about reconciling these contradictory elements? There is no easy answer. The trustees have to arrive at a consensus regarding how much risk they are willing to bear in the near term. (This decision is the central aspect of investment policy, which we discussed in Session 2: setting the policy asset allocation. We'll return to it later in Session 5 on investment risk tolerance.) Depending on the membership of the investment committee, the answer may change. You will have to decide for yourself how much risk you will tolerate in fulfilling the Fund's mission and continue to discuss that point of view with the other trustees.

Keep in mind, Molly, that as a fiduciary, your willingness to take risk should relate to the circumstances of the Fund, the sponsor (the university), and the beneficiaries, not to your personal feelings about risk. Given the primary aspect of the Fund's mission, the trustees should be careful never to take so much risk as to endanger the benefit security of plan participants. And as the staff has witnessed numerous times, investment portfolios with high *equity* allocations may experience considerable declines in value, resulting in materially diminished funded ratios. As a result, contributions skyrocket. Yet, the history of capital markets indicates that equity investments far outperform fixed-income investments, so choosing not to hold sizable equity positions would present a large potential opportunity cost to the university.

Liabilities

The Fund is an ongoing entity from which the university expects to pay a stream of retirement benefits to plan participants for a long time. All the stakeholders in the Fund prefer to have one measure that summarizes the value of those future benefits payments today. To compute that number, the plan's actuaries estimate the future benefit payments to be made to each current plan participant. They base their calculations on the participants' wages, ages, and lengths of service today and the participants' estimated retirement dates and life expectancies. Reflecting the fact that a dollar paid tomorrow is worth less than a dollar paid today, the actuaries then take into account the time value of the future pension payments by applying a market-based discount rate to the estimated payments. The sum of these discounted payments is the single dollar amount that, if invested today at that discount rate, could finance all the estimated benefit payments currently owed to the plan participants. The plan's actuaries refer to that single dollar amount as the plan's liabilities. (Public pension plans are required by the U.S. Governmental Accounting Standards Board to use a discount rate equal to the assumed expected return on fund assets. Private-sector pension plans, in contrast, are required to use a discount rate based on the yields of high-quality corporate bonds.)

The plan's liabilities, thus derived from the discounted future benefit payments, can be compared directly with the Fund's assets to determine how well funded the DB pension plan is. As we discussed, the funded ratio equals the Fund's assets divided by the plan's liabilities.

In a very real sense, the plan's liabilities are a form of debt. The university has made legal promises to pay the plan participants their retirement benefits. In lieu of giving them additional cash compensation today, the university has implicitly substituted a series of future payments. As a result, you can think of the liabilities as a nonmarketable bond issued to plan participants. The participants' deferred compensation equates to the "purchase price" of this pension bond. The pension payments represent the principal and interest payments made on the bond. Like any bond, this pension bond's value depends on the level of interest rates—in particular, the discount rate used to discount the estimated benefit payments. A change in that discount rate can have a large impact on the pension bond's value and hence on the value of the plan's liabilities.

The value of the plan's liabilities can, of course, change in ways beyond the effect of variations in the discount rate. As the university adds participants to the plan, or as the participants' income and service with the university grow, so will the plan's liabilities grow. The investment staff periodically works with the plan's actuaries to prepare a report on the size of the existing liabilities in light of the best available information at that time.

These concepts of liabilities and funded status apply to endowment and foundation funds as much as to DB pension plans. However, you won't find a *liability* value reported for the university's foundation and endowment funds that is comparable to what you find for the DB pension plan. The DB pension plan's liabilities, despite relying on a number of estimated inputs, are determined through a formulaic valuation process, whereas the foundation's and endowment's liabilities are not.

The benefit payments of the foundation and endowment are determined by these two funds' spending policies—the percentage of the Funds' assets that are paid out each year to beneficiaries. Those spending policies are based on such factors as peer practices, competition for donors, intergenerational equity (today's spenders versus tomorrow's), and perhaps most importantly, expectations regarding long-term inflation-adjusted returns available in the capital markets. Payments to the endowment and foundation beneficiaries will vary over time in ways that are difficult to forecast. As the Funds' asset values fluctuate, given the relatively fixed spending rates, so also do the payouts change.

Foundation and endowment beneficiaries expect to receive future benefit payments that, at the very least, are stable in real (inflation-adjusted) terms. This expectation is in contrast to the fixed nominal (unadjusted for inflation) benefit payments that are legally obligated in the case of most pension plans. This difference between real and nominal liabilities causes the objectives and strategies used for investing the university's foundation and endowment assets to differ significantly from the objectives and strategies used for investing the DB pension plan's assets.

Contributions

The university has established a *funding policy* for the DB pension plan that determines the timing and amount of contributions to the plan. That funding policy sets thresholds for the funded ratio that trigger consideration of contributions. The university has broad discretion regarding the specifics of contributions. (Private-sector plan sponsors are more constrained in terms of minimum contributions they must make.) The funded ratio thresholds set by the university are meant to be advisory in nature. In determining its funding policy, the university's administration weighs the relative importance of keeping the funded ratio near 100 percent against the importance of conserving cash for other university purposes. (For private-sector sponsors, the tax-advantaged nature of the pension fund also plays a role in determining funding policy. Contributions are tax deductible and investment earnings in the pension fund go untaxed, so a company may choose at times to "prefund" future benefit obligations by making contributions today instead of when the obligations are incurred.)

Three factors affect the funded ratio and may trigger the need for the university to make contributions. First, as discussed, the liabilities of a pension plan grow as the number of participants and their years of service grow, so the funding policy must consider how to fund these increases in liabilities. Second, as we also mentioned, changes in the discount rate may cause the DB pension plan's liabilities to increase or decrease over time. Third, the Fund may, depending on the returns earned by the Fund, grow or decrease.

To the extent that the investment committee holds equity and equitylike securities in the Fund, the Fund's value will grow in good markets and the benefit security ratio will improve, reducing the need for contributions. In poor markets, the Fund's value will decline, depressing the funded ratio and creating a need for contributions just at a time when the university's ability to make such contributions may be diminished.

In such difficult economic periods, discount rates may also be declining, which would push up the value of liabilities and have a negative impact on the funded ratio. This confluence of declining assets and rising liabilities has occurred twice in the first decade of this century. It accentuated the conflict in the Fund's mission between holding assets with high expected returns in order to lower financing costs and holding assets with lower expected returns to avoid severe fluctuations in the funded ratio and in contributions.

Previously, when we spoke of governance structure, we referred to the notion of a three-legged stool. We can use the same analogy here to conclude our discussion of the Fund's mission. This analogy applies whether a fund is associated with a private or public DB pension plan, an endowment, a foundation, or any pool of assets for which there are beneficiaries and for which there has been and may continue to be a source of contributions. Broadly speaking, three types of policies control the management of a pool of assets: investment policy, which defines the level of investment risk required to meet return objectives; funding policy, which defines the level and source of contributions into a fund; and benefit policy, which defines the amounts and timing of pension benefits. (For an endowment or foundation, as discussed, benefit policy is usually referred to as spending policy, which determines the amount to be distributed to the beneficiary entities.) Our conversations focus, of course, on investment policy. Nevertheless, the financial health of a pension, endowment, foundation, insurance company, or any other trust depends on all three policies.

Takeaways

- The primary aspect of a fund's mission is to have enough assets to pay all promised or expected benefits when due.
- A fund's mission should recognize the interests of all stakeholders, particularly those providing the benefits, those making contributions, and those receiving benefits from the fund.
- The best single measure of a fund's financial health is the funded ratio, defined as the ratio of fund assets to fund liabilities.
- Various aspects of a fund's mission can come into conflict with one another.
- The primary conflict is between reducing volatility in the funded ratio and contributions and keeping the costs of financing benefits low.
- Plan liabilities equal the present (or discounted) value of all future benefits expected to be paid to plan beneficiaries.
- The most important variable in calculating liabilities is the discount rate: The value of liabilities is inversely related to discount rate.
- The set of directives determining the amount and timing of payments to beneficiaries is called "benefits policy."
- The timing and amount of contributions to a fund are determined by a set of formal and informal rules called "funding policy."

QUESTIONS MOLLY SHOULD ASK

- When was the last time the mission for our DB pension fund was thoroughly reviewed? For our endowment fund? For our foundation? What was the outcome of these reviews?
- Who do we consider to be the primary stakeholders for the funds for which our investment committee has responsibility? How do we engage the stakeholders and understand their opinions?
- How is funding policy and benefit policy set for our various funds? Who are the parties responsible for these policies, and how do we interact with them?
- Are any significant changes anticipated regarding benefit policy or funding policy for any of our funds?
- How do we define the liabilities for our various funds, and how do we assess their funded status?

The DB pension fund

- What range in the funded ratio do we feel comfortable with for our pension plan? By how much should the funded ratio be allowed to fall below 1.0? How sensitive are we to fluctuations in its level?

- What is the current funded ratio of the pension plan, and how has it fluctuated over time?
- How do the trustees view the conflict between benefit security and lower funding costs for our pension plan?
- How sensitive are our pension liabilities to changes in the discount rate?
- Does the university have sufficient resources and liquidity to make contributions to our pension fund if the funded ratio should fall below a minimum threshold?
- Is the pension plan open to new participants? If not, have benefit accruals been frozen for current participants? If the plan is closed to new participants and new benefit accruals, how has that status redefined the Fund's mission?
- Do we have strategies in place to protect the pension plan's funded ratio from fluctuations in liability values caused by interest rate changes?

The endowment and foundation funds

- How do the endowment and foundation define their liabilities?
- Do the endowment and foundation take a relatively long-term or a short-term view when it comes to setting their funds' missions? What considerations have gone into making those decisions?
- What are the projected net cash flows of the endowment and foundation? Do fund-raising efforts provide material cash inflows?
- What expectations do the university's financial managers have regarding the endowment and foundation spending rates?

The DC investment options

- Do we view the DC pension plan as the primary source of retirement income for our employees or as a secondary source?
- What are the primary considerations that go into selecting investment options?
- Is our philosophy on investment options that plan participants should have a wide range of choices or that they should be offered a narrow range of choices that represent our best thinking?

Session 4. Investment Objectives

> You must have long-range goals to keep you
> from being frustrated by short-range failures.
>
> —*Charles C. Noble*

Molly, we now want to take the next step by declaring what the investment committee intends its investment program to accomplish—that is, what sort of investment outcomes would signal that the program has been successful. The trustees express those outcomes in a set of investment objectives.

Criteria for Effective Investment Objectives

The Fund's investment objectives contain both prospective and retrospective elements. In a prospective sense, the Fund's investment objectives assist in defining the structure of the investment program. The investment staff stays mindful of the established investment objectives when it implements the asset allocation policy and manager selection. The Fund's mission, on the one hand, provides a high-level sense of direction. The Fund's investment objectives, on the other hand, offer considerably more detail than the Fund's mission about the path that the investment committee expects the staff to follow. The objectives provide specific guidance regarding the critical trade-off between expected reward and risk that is reflected in the Fund's investment policy.

In a retrospective sense, the Fund's investment objectives play an important role in the assessment of the investment program's results. The Fund's investment objectives are part of the feedback-and-control mechanism embedded in the performance evaluation process. If the investment program fails to achieve the Fund's investment objectives, then it loses credibility and may bring about changes; if the investment program succeeds in achieving the Fund's investment objectives, then current practices are reinforced.

In contrast to the Fund's mission, which involves a set of broad purposes, the Fund's investment objectives are a quantifiable set of investment results that the investment committee expects to achieve over specified time periods. Therefore, investment objectives should meet several criteria. They should be

- unambiguous and measurable,
- specified in advance,
- actionable and attainable,
- reflective of the investment committee's risk tolerance, and

- consistent with the Fund's mission.

Let's consider each of these criteria.

Unambiguous and Measurable. Simply put, the investment committee attempts to be clear about what it expects the staff to accomplish when investing the Fund's assets. Therefore, the trustees develop unambiguous and measurable goals. Subjective or difficult-to-measure objectives typically result in confusion and are open to conflicting interpretations. In the end, they are often ignored, to everyone's consternation. For example, statements such as "the fund should generate returns commensurate with the risk assumed" are of little value in selecting investments or in determining whether the investment results were indeed satisfactory. These types of objectives fall under the category of "do good and avoid evil." Obviously, no one can argue with their positive intent, but they are more aspirational than practical.

In contrast, investment objectives expressed in clearly defined terms, particularly relative to a specified benchmark, help the staff design an effective investment program and allow the investment committee to evaluate the program's performance. For example, one of the Fund's investment objectives is to add 100–200 basis points (bps) annually of active management value while taking no more than 300–400 bps annually in aggregate active management risk in the U.S. equity asset class, evaluated over a five-year period. (A basis point is 1/100 of 1 percent, so 200 bps equals 2 percent.) The staff can clearly comprehend and discuss this objective and measure results relative to it. The objective dictates how the staff constructs the lineup of U.S. equity managers. It obviously necessitates hiring active managers, and it also requires relatively aggressive active managers. In addition, the objective affects how the staff combines the managers into a portfolio of managers. Furthermore, as the staff analysts prepare performance evaluation reports for the investment committee, they structure those reports to provide information as to what the Fund's U.S. equity managers have done relative to this objective and why the desired outcome has or has not occurred.

Specified in Advance. The investment committee defines the Fund's investment objectives in advance of the time period over which the investment program is held accountable to those objectives. To do otherwise would run the risk of revisionist analysis, a truly dangerous activity from a governance standpoint. Whether it is the investment committee critiquing the investment staff or outsiders evaluating the decisions of the trustees, investment objectives defined after the evaluation period has ended are contentious and fundamentally unfair. The process of investing, because it produces measurable results, is always open to unconstructive second guessing, regardless of what preventive practices the trustees put into effect. It thus makes little sense for the trustees to compound the problem by delineating expected outcomes prior to the investment activity taking place and then holding the staff responsible for other outcomes not communicated until later. Molly, you certainly realize that, although all decision makers have a responsibility to be aware of changes in the environment and recommend modifications when necessary, in the conduct of business affairs, you don't instruct someone to do A and then wonder why he or she didn't do B.

Actionable and Attainable. The investment committee sets actionable and attainable fund investment objectives. The staff must be able to influence, in some way, the outcomes that are being evaluated in light of the objectives. Investment objectives that cannot be acted upon produce frustration and a sense of powerlessness on the part of the staff. Instead of being an incentive to drive the investment program in a particular direction, those types of objectives can generate a bunker mentality with staff members fearful that they will be held accountable for results over which they have no control.

At many organizations, investment objectives come stated in the form of absolute return targets, which in many cases are not actionable. Consider a common objective: Earn a return in excess of the liability discount rate of 8 percent. Rarely are investment products available that offer a guaranteed fixed return of 8 percent. Still, over the very long term, that objective might appear attainable. With sufficiently aggressive investments in equities, an investment program could have achieved that result over certain long historical periods. There have also been many extended periods, however, when the capital markets simply did not produce returns of that magnitude. In those periods, that absolute return target was not actionable. Nothing the staff at those funds could do would have achieved that goal.

Investment objectives expressed relative to investable benchmarks, such as a *market index*, are more likely to be actionable. (We will talk more about benchmarks in Session 7 on performance evaluation.) Superior active management programs, for example, can be expected to outperform appropriate benchmarks regardless of the market environment. Thus, a realistic return objective for active managers should focus the staff on hiring the most productive managers. Staff members can feel confident that if they do their jobs effectively, the intended result can be achieved.

The trustees should design investment objectives for the Fund that also are attainable. Although an investment objective involving a return relative to a particular benchmark might be actionable, to state that the Fund's active managers should produce active results 500 bps above the benchmark is unrealistic. In setting attainable investment objectives, the trustees should review what other investment programs have been able to accomplish and what the capital markets and investment managers have offered investors over varying time periods.

Attainable investment objectives also avoid unrealistic precision. The investment committee prefers objectives involving a range of desired outcomes as opposed to a single numeric target. Such a range better captures the trustees' understanding of the variability inherent in investment management.

Reflective of the Investment Committee's Risk Tolerance. The Fund's investment objectives should reflect the risk tolerance of the trustees in pursuing the Fund's mission. The investment committee has to feel comfortable with the investment objectives that it establishes. As a trustee, Molly, you need to understand the amount of risk that those objectives will lead the investment program to pursue. Investment objectives that translate into an aggressive investment program may produce uncomfortable results in periods of poor market performance. You have to be able to tolerate those results. Suppose the investment objective calls for high positive real rates of return and thus a large allocation to equities. If the trustees decide *after* a period of significantly negative returns in the stock market that they cannot bear the risk, the consequences will be counterproductive, potentially producing a "buy high, sell low" outcome.

Consistent with the Fund's Mission. The investment committee has designed the Fund's mission to be consistent with the trustees' collective risk tolerance. Because the investment objectives should also reflect that level of risk tolerance, it follows that if the Fund achieves its investment objectives, then the Fund's mission will similarly be fulfilled. At first, that logic might seem obvious, but it is quite easy to end up with investment objectives that convey different messages from what one might understand from the Fund's mission. For example, suppose the Fund's mission strongly emphasizes maintaining a funded ratio at or above full funding, with little tolerance for volatility in that ratio. Establishing an investment objective that involved taking considerable risk in the pursuit of returns higher than those necessary to maintain full funding would be inconsistent with the Fund's mission.

Examples of Investment Objectives

To give you a sense of what constitutes viable investment objectives and what does not, we have provided in **Exhibit 1** some examples of what other organizations have used. Some of the examples are valid investment objectives. Other examples, despite being widely accepted, actually violate many of the criteria for acceptability.

Exhibit 1. Examples of Investment Objectives

Investment Objective	Comment	Assessment
Achieve an investment return in excess of the policy asset mix's return over a five-year time period.	Actionable and attainable by use of active management. Consistent with the trustees' willingness to bear risk and the fund's mission. Unambiguous. Specified in advance.	Good
Generate active management performance in excess of an appropriate benchmark over a five-year time period.	Actionable and attainable by use of active management. Consistent with the trustees' willingness to bear risk and the fund's mission. Unambiguous. Specified in advance.	Good
Maintain a funded ratio (assets/liabilities) in excess of 0.9 measured annually.	Appropriate for funds in which liabilities or expected fund outflows have been specified (e.g., defined-benefit plans, insurance companies). Actionable and attainable as long as the fund has access to source of contributions. Unambiguous. Specified in advance.	Good
Realize investment performance that allows annual spending or fund withdrawals to equal or grow relative to the prior year's spending.	Pertains primarily to endowments and foundations. Based on the idea that fund beneficiaries have an aversion to declines in benefits.	Good
Maintain projected investment risk consistent with investment policy specifications.	Acknowledges the existence of different types of investment risk and a policy to incur certain ones, in approved amounts. Actionable and attainable.	Good
Outperform the returns of the median fund in a peer group universe.	Ambiguous and not actionable (median fund is unknown); possibly inconsistent with the trustees' willingness to bear risk or the fund's mission.	Poor
Attain return (equal to or greater than) the actuarial rate of return.	Possibly achievable over a long time period but certainly not annually.	Poor
Attain return (equal to or greater than) S&P 500 Index + 3 percent.	Unlikely to be attainable; possibly inconsistent with the trustees' willingness to bear risk.	Poor
No negative investment performance years.	Achievable only with low-risk, low-return investments that are likely to be inconsistent with the fund's mission and investment policy.	Bad
Attain U.S. Consumer Price Index + 3 percent.	Not actionable. No such investable alternative exists. Purely aspirational.	Bad
"Beat Harvard."	Not actionable (Harvard's investment policy and process is not known) and not necessarily consistent with the trustees' willingness to bear risk or the fund's mission. Purely aspirational.	Bad

Takeaways

- A fund's investment objectives are a quantifiable set of investment results that decision makers expect to achieve over specified time periods.
- Investment objectives play both a prospective and retrospective role in directing the investment program.
- A fund's investment objectives should be unambiguous and measurable, specified in advance, actionable and attainable, reflective of decision makers' risk tolerance, and consistent with the fund's mission.
- The most useful investment objectives generally are those expressed relative to an investable alternative (such as a market index).
- Investment objectives are best specified as a range of desirable outcomes as opposed to a single number.

QUESTIONS MOLLY SHOULD ASK

- What are the Fund's investment objectives? When were they last reviewed?
- If the investment objectives are attained, do we expect that the Fund's mission will likewise be achieved?
- Are the investment committee and staff satisfied that all of our investment objectives meet the criteria of being actionable and attainable?
- Have there been times in the past when poor performance or turbulent markets caused the trustees to question the Fund's investment objectives? Discuss those situations.
- Has the investment committee modified the investment objectives over time to reflect changes made to the investment program? If so, describe those changes.
- Are the Fund's investment objectives consistent with the trustees' collective risk tolerance?
- Do the Fund's investment management strategies (for example, policy asset allocation, active versus passive management) appropriately reflect its investment objectives?
- Are the Fund's investment objectives integrated into the reporting for purposes of performance evaluation?
- How has the investment program performed relative to the Fund's investment objectives?

Session 5. Investment Risk Tolerance

> I think we should follow a simple rule:
> If we can take the worst, take the risk.
>
> —*Dr. Joyce Brothers*

Novice investors commonly focus on returns and give only passing consideration to risk. Even sophisticated investors are prone to this myopia at times. Molly, you've probably observed this phenomenon simply by reading mainstream financial press reports reviewing investment results at year-end. These articles highlight the star performers and invariably display the top managers' performances only in terms of returns. The stories make no reference to the amount of risk the managers took in the pursuit of those stellar outcomes.

Return Is Only Half the Story

The cause of this serious and persistent oversight should come as no surprise to you. *Investment returns* are a tangible, after-the-fact concept. The trustees and staff can clearly see the effect of returns as they periodically examine the Fund's asset statement. Investment risk, however, is an intangible, before-the-fact idea. Its impact on the Fund's value can be only vaguely discerned by observing the volatility of that value over time. Risk involves the notion of a range of possible investment values in the future. But in the end, the Fund has one and only one value, and that value is generated by its investment return. In that sense, we actually experience returns but we only predict risk.

Yet, in fulfilling your duties as a trustee, risk plays a much more important role than do returns. Returns are the past; risk is the future. The investment committee can attempt to influence the direction of the Fund only in the future, not in the past. Benjamin Graham, the father of security analysis, once said, "The essence of investment management entails the management of risk, not the management of returns." The trustees can't control the Fund's returns, Molly, but it is your responsibility to manage risk by ensuring that robust investment policies and processes are in place, with proper controls, accountability, oversight, and reporting.

Types of Investment Risk

From the trustees' perspective, investment risk ultimately refers to the possibility of not achieving the Fund's investment objectives and mission or, more generally, not being able to provide the Fund's beneficiaries with the benefits that they expect or have been promised. A variety of investment risks can affect the success of the investment program. The investment committee has chosen to bear some of these risks purposely because it expects to earn a return commensurate with the *uncertainty* in outcomes caused by those risks. The trustees have attempted to identify and minimize other risks, those for which they expect to receive no reward.

The primary types of investment risks to which the trustees intentionally expose the Fund fall into three primary categories:

- capital market risk,
- active management risk, and
- liquidity risk.

First, *capital market risk* arises because investing in the capital markets (for example, the stock and bond markets) brings with it an uncertainty in returns caused by a common sensitivity of the markets to broad economic events. When the economy is doing well, all risky financial assets tend to benefit to some degree, and it is the opposite situation when the economy is doing poorly. Because, as a whole, investors in the capital markets cannot avoid this sensitivity, they will hold these risky assets only if they are paid to do so. The investment committee expects that the markets will reward long-term investors who bear this capital market risk.

The second risk that the investment committee expects to be rewarded for bearing is *active management risk*. We introduced this type of risk in our discussion of governance structure in Session 1. The term refers to the uncertainty of a manager's performance relative to the manager's benchmark. We'll talk more about passive and active management in our next session, but for the moment, recall that passive managers expect to generate performance roughly equal to that of their benchmarks. Active managers, on the other hand, produce returns that are different (either positively or negatively) from their benchmarks' returns. The difference in a manager's performance from that of the benchmark is referred to as *active management return*. The trustees are willing to incur the uncertainty associated with this active management return because they believe that the staff can identify managers with *investment skill* who will generate performance, over time, in excess of their benchmarks.

The third compensated source of investment risk is *liquidity risk*. For example, the Fund invests in various forms of private equity that, in many respects, are similar to the Fund's common stock investments, but the private equity holdings are much more illiquid. The investment committee invests in private equity partly because the trustees believe that the market will pay an incremental return to investors willing to take the chance that they will not be able to quickly convert the value of their private equity investments into cash.

Other investment risks create uncertainty in the Fund's investment performance, but for those risks, the investment committee does not expect any return as compensation. For example, if the staff is not careful how assets are allocated to the investment managers, then they may introduce "style bias" (that is, an undesirable concentration of assets in a particular investment strategy, such as small company *growth stocks*) that can have a material impact on the Fund's returns in a particular asset class. The trustees have no reason to expect to be rewarded, however, for bearing that type of risk. As a consequence, the investment committee has directed the staff to minimize exposures to this risk and other forms of uncompensated risk as cost-effectively as it can.

Measuring Risk

How do we quantify risk? Some practitioners don't even try. They contend that investment risk is too dynamic and subtle a concept to summarize numerically. They prefer to rely on intuition, experience, and rules of thumb to control investment risk. The Freedonia University Investment Committee has directed the staff to attempt to define risk quantitatively, although the committee members realize the inherent difficulties of doing so and thus never blindly rely on numerical estimates. However, it doesn't matter whether one uses a qualitative process, quantitative process, or a mix of the two. What is crucial is that the process be structured, comprehensive, and proactive rather than *ad hoc*, narrow, and reactive.

The investment staff's risk quantification process begins with an estimation of the distribution of potential returns for the investments under consideration. That distribution describes the range and associated probability of various outcomes. Typically, the staff uses historical return information to provide the starting point for estimating this return distribution. From there, the staff calculates the distribution's *standard deviation*, which measures the size of fluctuations around the distribution's most likely, or expected, value. High-risk investments tend to be more volatile than low-risk investments and will have a wider dispersion of outcomes (hence, a larger standard deviation). For a normal (bell-shaped) distribution, the standard deviation fully describes the dispersion of the return distribution and is a key descriptor of investment risk.

For example, consider an investment in common stocks compared with an investment in government bonds. Stocks may conceivably lose their entire value, but they may also increase several multiples in value. U.S. government bonds, however, although they may decline in value in the near term because of increases in interest rates, will never explicitly default—or at least we hope not. Similarly, although government bonds may temporarily rise in value because of a fall in interest rates, they will never return more at maturity than their principal value. As a result, government bonds are less risky than common stocks; the standard deviation of common stock returns is greater than the standard deviation of government bond returns.

Of course, what the staff is really looking for is a measure of the size and frequency of potential losses, especially large losses, not simply a measure of volatility. Certainly, there are numerous conceptual problems involved in using standard deviation as the measure of risk. Indeed, you should be skeptical, Molly, of any single statistic used to summarize risk. For example, you should question whether investment returns are normally distributed; if not, standard deviation could be a poor gauge of risk. The returns on some types of investments, such as options, most certainly are not normally distributed. One can make the case that returns on even such "plain vanilla" investments as stocks and bonds are not normally distributed. Moreover, standard deviation doesn't differentiate between upside and downside results; it only measures volatility, and volatility is not risk. Still, despite its flaws, for largely practical reasons, standard deviation has long maintained its place as a primary risk metric. Virtually all the reports you will see from investment managers and the staff will use standard deviation as the most common risk measure.

Risk involves the chance of loss taken with the hope of earning an acceptable profit. More precisely, risk incorporates both the probability and the magnitude of potential loss. Some practitioners, therefore, express risk by using both standard deviation and a measure of the size of the investment (such as dollars invested). The combination of the two factors is used to create a risk metric called "value at risk" (VaR), which indicates the amount that the investor might lose, at a minimum, with a given probability (for example, a 5 percent chance of losing at least $10 million).

The staff also estimates risk by conducting *stress tests* that evaluate the potential impact of adverse investment environments on the Fund's investments. Other practitioners focus on more intricate measures of risk that characterize the return distribution in complex ways, but those measures are well beyond what we can cover in this session.

Relationship between Risk and Expected Return

As you are probably aware, risk and expected return tend to go together. That is, investments with high risk levels will typically have high *expected* returns. Why? Well, it is generally assumed that investors as a group tend to prefer less risk to more risk for the same expected return. Molly, suppose you were asked to choose between an investment with a guaranteed 8 percent return or one with an expected 8 percent return but a chance to earn between 4 percent or 12 percent. Most likely, you'd take the certain return. You probably can be enticed to own riskier investments only if you anticipate earning higher returns. You would give up the guaranteed 8 percent return only if the risky investment had an expected return higher than 8 percent.

It makes sense that this relationship should hold true. That is, if investors truly dislike risk, then the greater the potential for loss associated with the risky investment, the more return investors will demand (or expect) in order to hold that security or a portfolio of those securities. Notice we don't say that the greater the potential for loss, the more return investors *will* earn. If a riskier investment always had a greater return, then it wouldn't be risky. So, the extra reward on a risky investment has to be prospective, and the possibility must exist that the extra payoff may not actually occur.

This relationship between risk and expected returns is observed when we examine historical capital market returns. Asset classes with higher standard deviations (such as common stocks) actually have earned higher returns over reasonably long periods of time than have asset classes with lower standard deviations (such as government bonds). In any given month or year, bonds can and do outperform stocks, sometimes by considerable margins, but when we look at returns over decades, we see that the capital markets have rewarded taking on risk.

Managing Risk through Diversification

There are ways to directly insure some types of investments against certain types of losses, but this insurance involves paying a hefty premium. A much cheaper and simpler technique to protect against risk is *diversification*—building a portfolio out of investments whose returns do not move in the same direction at the same time (that is, whose returns are not highly positively correlated).

The old saying, "Don't put all your eggs in one basket," alludes to the wisdom of diversification. Suppose you have two assets, A and B, with the same expected return and the same risk. If their returns don't always move in lockstep, then the combination of the two has the same expected return but a lower risk than either one of the two assets individually. Bad things happening to Asset A tend to be offset at the same time by good things happening to Asset B, and vice versa. Adding *uncorrelated* asset classes to a fund tends to reduce the fund's risk. For this reason, many funds include real estate, *commodities*, distressed bonds, and so on, in addition to stocks and bonds in their investment programs. Finding and managing low-correlated or uncorrelated asset classes is not simple and has numerous potential pitfalls, but the benefits can be substantial.

Diversification has been referred to as the one "free lunch" in investing. Of course, after the fact, it will turn out that one asset had a higher return than the others, so if you had known that outcome in advance, you wouldn't have diversified. In that sense, the lunch isn't really free. But as noted when we began this discussion, investment management is about managing risk, not managing return.

As a trustee, Molly, you should assure yourself that the investment staff at Freedonia University has taken full advantage of available diversification opportunities. You should inquire about concentrated allocations to particular asset classes or even individual investments and question the assumptions behind those decisions. When the staff requests to add new asset classes, you should question whether the staff has considered how those investments correlate with the Fund's existing investments and whether their addition improves the Fund's diversification.

But beware on two counts. First, many asset classes seem to display a low *correlation* with one another in normal economic environments. When the market climate turns sour, however, some of these asset classes actually experience high correlations, thereby producing negligible diversification benefits. For example, in economic expansions, high-yield debt acts like other bonds; in recessions, it acts more like equity, which severely diminishes its diversification value. As a result, there is a saying that "the only things that go up in a down market are correlations." Still, cash and government bonds usually do go up in value in a down market for stocks because cash and bonds are perceived as safe havens. It is important, therefore, not to overlook these "boring, old-fashioned" asset classes.

Second, some asset classes that appear to be good diversifiers involve considerable costs, in terms of both management and transaction expenses, and they may be illiquid as well. The benefits of the diversification they offer can be outweighed by the cost drag on investment returns.

Diversification offers a simple and generally low-cost means of managing investment risk. It requires no special knowledge of the trustees' collective risk tolerance or the Fund's investment objectives. As a result, it is a widely used risk-control procedure. However, many funds have deployed more sophisticated techniques of managing their risk levels while targeting expected returns. Those methods have become widely referred to as *"risk budgeting."*

Risk Budgeting

The ability to bear risk is a scarce resource in the same way that capital (i.e., money) is a scarce resource. Thus, risk should be allocated to investments that offer the most return for the amount of the resource (risk) invested. The investment committee budgets, or allocates, capital to various investments. The same amount of capital can be invested in a six-month U.S. T-bill or a *venture capital* start-up with considerably different consequences for the Fund. As a result, you can see that the trustees are allocating more than simply dollars; they are really allocating risk. The idea of risk budgeting requires quantifying the risk of various types of investments and combinations of investments. This process allows the trustees and staff to use a common language, or metric, for allocating risk, measuring whether too much or too little risk has been allocated, and comparing actual results with expectations.

Through the risk-budgeting process, the investment staff can decide beforehand how much individual security risk to allow, how much capital to give any one manager, how much of the portfolio to hold in particular asset classes, and so on. Risk budgeting permits the staff to evaluate trade-offs in terms of risk and expected return between available portfolio choices. The amount of risk that the staff budgets to any particular investment (for example, an asset class or a manager) should have a close relationship to the expected return on that investment. Indeed, part of the value added by a risk management program is to help frame investment decisions in terms of the return required to justify taking on a particular type of risk.

Risk budgeting involves the use of quantitative risk models that provide insight regarding allocations to asset classes, managers, and even individual investments. Inputs into these models often include estimates of the standard deviations of the available asset classes, the correlations among those asset classes, and the returns expected to be produced by those asset classes. The output of a risk model is a set of allocations to asset classes and/or managers within asset classes that are expected to produce returns and risks consistent with the trustees' preferences.

Investment Risk Tolerance

We have taken a roundabout way to get to the subject of this session—namely, investment risk tolerance. Perhaps the most important part of managing risk is the human element. The markets are unpredictable in unpredictable ways. There will always be more unknowns and chaos to confound us. Molly, your risk tolerance reflects your ability to handle the ups and downs of markets and their impact on the Fund. High risk tolerance doesn't mean you can watch market volatility without emotion. Rather, it means that in those periods when markets are volatile and serious losses are occurring, you are likely to be confident that the capital markets do reward patient risk takers over the long run. Low risk tolerance implies that you are uncomfortable with market volatility and would prefer to forgo higher expected returns in exchange for more predictability and reduced chances of serious losses.

Why is investment risk tolerance important? As we discussed, expected returns are directly related to risk. The higher the returns that the investment committee targets for the Fund, the more risk the Fund will have to incur. The trustees implement their decisions primarily through their choice of the Fund's policy asset mix. Consultants and the staff can offer you and the other trustees advice regarding the risk level needed to achieve the Fund's investment objectives. In the end, however, only the trustees can establish the appropriate risk level for the Fund and only the trustees collectively must be able to tolerate that risk level. If the investment committee sets a risk level for the Fund inconsistent with what the trustees are capable of bearing, then bad decisions will invariably be made at the worst possible times. When market volatility hits the Fund and significant losses occur, the trustees don't want to fall victim to fear and propose reducing risk at the wrong time. To sell at the bottom, out of an inability to contemplate further losses, simply locks in those losses and makes it much less likely that the Fund can recover.

Molly, you should understand the difference between your personal risk tolerance and the investment committee's risk tolerance. Your own investment time horizon and financial situation undoubtedly differ from those of the Fund. As a trustee, you must be able to set aside your personal concerns and focus on what is best for the Fund over the long run. Consequently, it is likely that the risk level that the investment committee assigns to the Fund will differ from what you would apply to your personal portfolio, whether that involves more or less risk in the Fund than in your portfolio.

We can't easily quantify risk tolerance. As a trustee, you may be asked to provide opinions as to the maximum volatility in the Fund's returns that you would accept or the maximum loss that you might be willing to experience over a year or multiyear period. Aggregated across the investment committee, the answers help convey a sense of how much risk the trustees can bear. In the final analysis, however, no formula can determine the trustees' collective risk tolerance and the associated "right" policy asset mix to achieve the Fund's investment objectives. The staff and the consultants will portray the range of investment outcomes associated with any particular asset strategy, but it is up to the trustees to imagine how they, as a group, would feel in a market crisis and, more importantly, to imagine how they should—or shouldn't—react.

Takeaways

- Investors often focus largely on returns and fail to consider the risk involved in generating those returns.
- A fund's decision makers purposely take on certain investment risks with an expectation of receiving a positive return over time. A fund's primary investment risks are capital market risk, active management risk, and liquidity risk.
- Additional risks for which there is not an expected return can have a material impact on an investment program. These risks should be identified and minimized.
- Quantifying investment risk usually begins with an examination of historical returns and a calculation of the dispersion (often expressed as the standard deviation) of the distribution of those returns.
- Higher expected returns are associated with higher risk. Investors need to be compensated for bearing more uncertainty with an expectation of realizing higher returns.
- The simplest and cheapest way to manage risk is through adequate diversification.
- Asset classes whose returns display low or zero correlations are attractive because when combined, they enhance diversification and reduce a fund's risk.
- Risk is a scarce resource that should be managed carefully. Some fund sponsors do so through formal risk-budgeting processes that quantify the trade-off between risk and expected return.
- Risk management is like any other management process: It involves thinking about what might happen and what to do if bad things happen.
- Risk budgeting involves evaluating the trade-off between risk and expected return of various combinations of investments.
- Risk tolerance indicates an investor's ability to bear losses in the pursuit of higher returns. A fund's decision makers need to be able to set aside their personal concerns and arrive at a collective risk tolerance for the fund that is consistent with the fund's mission and investment objectives.

QUESTIONS MOLLY SHOULD ASK

- What risks do I face as a fiduciary?
- What are the most important risks faced by the Fund? Who is responsible for managing each of them? What are we doing (or not doing) to mitigate those risks?

- Do we have an established process for identifying, quantifying, and managing investment risk?
- Who on the investment staff is responsible for our risk management efforts?
- Do we engage in any formal type of risk budgeting? If so, what is that process? If not, why not?
- Does our risk management focus only on the Fund's assets, or does it also take into account the Fund's liabilities?
- Given the current investment policy, how much could the Fund lose in a "worst-case" scenario?
- What market events could cause serious liquidity concerns for the Fund?
- In what areas of the investment program, if any, do we purposely concentrate our investments, and what is the rationale for doing so?
- Is there a regular risk report to the investment committee that discusses each risk and the management/mitigation process?
- How do the Fund's consultants contribute to the risk management process?
- What types of discussions and studies have been carried out by the trustees, the staff, and the consultants to determine the investment committee's collective risk tolerance?
- Is there general agreement among the trustees that the level of risk in the Fund is consistent with the Fund's mission and investment objectives? Where has there been disagreement?

Session 6. Investment Assets

> Know thy opportunity.
>
> —*Pittacus*

The Freedonia University Investment Committee has chosen to invest the Fund in a variety of asset types. As we discussed in Session 2 on investment policy and Session 5 on investment risk tolerance, we refer to those asset types as "asset classes." Asset classes are simply collections of securities that have common attributes. Although the distinctions among asset classes are, admittedly, somewhat arbitrary, the designation of asset classes helps the trustees and the staff to develop intelligent approaches to setting the Fund's policy asset mix and the Fund's risk level. Without asset class distinctions, conversations among the trustees and the staff about how to implement the investment program would be cumbersome and unproductive.

Types of Investment Assets

Broadly, the investment committee has authorized investments in three primary asset classes: common stocks (also called "equities"), bonds (also called "fixed income" or "debt"), and so-called *alternative investments*. The trustees have further broken down these asset classes into additional asset classes. For example, the Fund holds U.S. common stocks and non-U.S. common stocks. Within the international common stock class, the Fund owns developed-market common stocks and emerging-market common stocks. Similarly, bond holdings can be segregated into U.S bonds and non-U.S. bonds, and each of these categories can be divided into investment-grade bonds and high-yield bonds.

Recall that Appendix B contains the Freedonia University DB pension fund's policy asset mix and provides an example of the various asset classes in which the investment committee has authorized the staff to invest. We won't have time in this session to consider each asset class (although we will discuss alternative investments in more detail later), but you can find a description of the Fund's asset classes in most standard investment textbooks.

Diversifying across Asset Classes

The investment committee's primary investment strategy is to diversify widely among risky assets. As discussed in the previous session, diversification offers a cost-free and simple means of controlling risk. The Fund does not invest in only one security. It invests in a portfolio of securities. The staff does not retain only one investment manager. The staff hires a group of investment managers using multiple investment approaches. And the managers do not invest in only one type of stock or bond. They invest across a wide spectrum of financial securities—from publicly traded stocks and bonds to a variety of less liquid investments that we categorize as alternative investments.

The Fund's potential *investable universe* of publicly traded stocks includes most equities that are traded in both U.S. and non-U.S. markets. That adds up to literally tens of thousands of securities. The Fund's investment managers will never own most of these stocks. For various reasons, such as size, liquidity, and lack of freely tradable shares, many of these stocks are not investable for all intents and purposes. Thus, the managers have to contend with an opportunity set that is much smaller than the potential universe.

The manner in which the staff approaches the Fund's investments in publicly traded bonds is quite similar to how it handles investments in publicly traded stocks. There are, however, subtle but important differences. Most notable is, as you know, that stocks are issued by corporations but bonds are issued not only by corporations but also by a wide variety of other organizations, including, to name a few, governments (state, local, and federal), agencies of government, and not-for-profit institutions. In addition to the many entities, there are numerous types of fixed-income securities that any one entity can issue. Whereas corporations typically issue one type of common stock, the many entities that issue bonds can also issue many different types of bonds or fixed-income securities, each backed by certain assets, maturing at different times, and with its own terms and conditions.

Market Indices

To understand the breadth and performance of the investable stock and bond universes, the trustees and staff turn to market indices that represent the publicly traded equity and fixed-income markets. These indices identify a large number of investable stocks and bonds that are representative of a particular market. A security's weight in the index is typically based on its *market capitalization* (share or bond price times number of shares or bonds outstanding) as a percentage of the total market capitalization of all the securities in the index. Inclusion in an index is usually determined by an objective set of rules or the decisions of a selection committee.

Perhaps the primary advantage of a market index is that it provides a performance history. By observing the returns earned by the index in the past, the trustees and staff get an indication of the risks and returns of the market that the index represents and the correlations of that market with other investments.

As we noted in Session 5 on investment risk tolerance, this historical information is valuable in developing the risk and return expectations used in setting a risk budget for the investment program. The indices also represent important accountability standards for assessing the Fund's performance, as we will discuss in Session 7 on performance evaluation.

For your convenience, **Exhibit 2** provides a list of commonly used equity and fixed-income market indices and their key characteristics. As you can see, in selecting an index to represent the Fund's investments in a particular asset class, the investment committee has a wide variety of choices. The market indices selected by the investment committee to represent the Fund's asset class investments are called the "asset class targets."

To examine how a particular asset class target is selected, let's look at the Fund's publicly traded equity investments as an example. The investment committee could adopt only one index, such as the All Country World Index, as a benchmark for all available stocks in both the U.S. market and the non-U.S. market, or it could treat these markets as separate asset classes and select one market index for U.S. stocks and one or more for non-U.S. stocks.

There is no one right answer. You'll find a variety of approaches at various funds. With the increasing globalization of investments, many funds have decided simply to refer to global equities in their policy asset mixes. As you can see in Appendix B, the policy asset mix chosen by the investment committee displays a combination of asset class targets for the U.S. equity, non-U.S. developed-market equity, and emerging-market equity investments.

The trustees' rationale for this approach was their familiarity with the U.S. equity market and the long history of investment performance available for these particular market indices, which allows a good understanding of their risk and return characteristics. The investment committee may revisit that decision in the future.

External and Internal Investment Management

After the investment committee establishes a structure for the Fund's public equities and fixed-income investments, the trustees need a strategy to implement the Fund's investments. Who will manage the investments and how the investments will be managed are two important questions.

Regarding the first question, the Fund's investments can be managed externally or internally. That is, the investment committee can instruct the staff to hire outside professional investment management firms or it can employ an on-site staff of investment professionals operating under the CIO. Most funds use external investment managers to some degree to manage their assets, and many have all of their assets managed externally. The Freedonia University

Exhibit 2. Sample of Widely Used Market Indices

Asset Class	Representative Benchmark	Description
Public equity		
U.S. equity	S&P 500 Index	500 blue-chip, mostly large-cap U.S. stocks
	Russell 2000 Index	2,000 small-cap U.S. stocks
	Russell 3000 Index	Largest 3,000 U.S. stocks by market cap (large, mid, and small)
Non-U.S. equity: Developed-market equity	MSCI World ex U.S. Index	Approximately 85 percent of the market cap of 22 developed-market equity markets, excluding the United States
	MSCI EAFE Index	Same as above but excluding Canada
Emerging-market equity	MSCI Emerging Markets Index	Includes approximately 85 percent of the market cap of 22 emerging-market equity markets
Global equity	MSCI All Country World Index	Combines developed- and emerging-market equity indices (including the United States)
Fixed income		
Core fixed income	Barclays Capital Aggregate Bond Index	Investment-grade, government-sponsored, corporate, mortgaged-backed bonds and other asset-backed securities, issued in U.S. dollars
High yield	Merrill Lynch U.S. High Yield Cash Pay Index	Debt securities issued by corporations rated lower than investment grade by one or more of the major rating agencies
Emerging-market debt	J.P. Morgan Emerging Markets Bond Index Global	Dollar-denominated debt securities issued by emerging-market countries
	J.P. Morgan Government Bond Index—Emerging Markets	Local-currency-denominated debt securities issued by emerging-market countries
Global sovereign debt	Citigroup World Government Bond Index	Sovereign bonds issued by 23 developed countries (all investment grade)
TIPS	Barclays Capital U.S. TIPS Index	All inflation-linked bonds issued by the U.S. Treasury
Alternative investments		
Real estate	FTSE EPRA/NAREIT Developed Index	All real estate investment trust (REIT) securities issued in developed markets in North America, Europe, and Asia
	NCREIF Property Index	A noninvestable index that tracks unlevered returns on more than 6,000 U.S. properties held by institutional investors in the office, retail, industrial, and apartment sectors

(continued)

Exhibit 2. Sample of Widely Used Market Indices (continued)

Asset Class	Representative Benchmark	Description
Private equity	Cambridge Associates U.S. Venture Capital Index	A noninvestable index based on return data compiled on funds representing more than three-quarters of the total dollars raised by venture capital managers since 1981
	Cambridge Associates Buyout Index	A noninvestable index based on return data compiled on funds representing more than two-thirds of the total dollars raised by leveraged buyout, subordinated debt, and special situations managers since 1986
Absolute return	HFRX Global Hedge Fund Index	A noninvestable non-value-weighted index of liquid, transparent hedge fund separate accounts engineered to achieve representative performance of a larger universe of hedge fund strategies
	HFRI Fund of Funds Composite Index	A noninvestable equally weighted index of more than 800 hedge funds of funds

Notes: HFR = Hedge Fund Research; NCREIF = National Council of Real Estate Investment Fiduciaries; MSCI = Morgan Stanley Capital International; TIPS = Treasury Inflation-Protected Securities. All indices are market-capitalization weighted unless indicated otherwise.

Investment Committee has chosen this latter approach. There are solid reasons to use internal investment management, primarily related to lower cost and more direct investment control. Those advantages are typically offset, however, by fewer degrees of freedom in making investment management changes and the large size of assets required to acquire top investment talent cost-effectively.

Employing external investment managers requires the investment committee to seek skillful external investment organizations. One of the downsides of using external managers is that their organizations change over time. Individuals come and go, and the organizations themselves undergo changes, sometimes being acquired by other investment management firms, sometimes even dissolving. This dynamic marketplace requires constant monitoring to ensure that the Fund's interests are protected. The investment staff spends a considerable amount of time on manager monitoring, often asking the Fund's investment consultant to assist in the process.

Of course, internal investment managers also come and go. Therefore, all funds that use internal management face the challenge of competing in the marketplace for qualified investment management talent. The compensation for internal managers is often too high for funds to accept on a staff level.

Furthermore, internal investment management requires considerable technology infrastructure and back-office support. In the end, external managers definitely are no cheaper, yet most funds prefer to pay external managers, who are also easier to dismiss than internal managers if performance is unacceptable.

Active and Passive Management

Directly related to the question of *who* will manage the Fund's investments is the issue of *how* the investments should be managed. In a broad sense, the investment committee has two choices. First, it could instruct the manager to invest the assets passively. That is, the manager could be directed to hold a portfolio designed to match the performance of a particular market index. This process is referred to as "*indexing.*" For example, the trustees could instruct the manager simply to match (or "index to") the performance of a market index representing the U.S. equity asset class.

Indexing is a simple, low-cost form of investment management. Essentially, the manager holds all or most of the securities contained in the market index in the same proportions as the securities are held in the index. A manager cannot match the performance of the index exactly for a variety of reasons, including trading costs and management fees. Nevertheless, passive management offers the promise that the Fund's investment results will always be near those of the selected market index, with little variation around the index return. In exchange for this consistency of results, of course, the trustees can never expect the passive manager's results to exceed the returns reported for the market index by any appreciable amount.

Alternatively, the investment committee could direct the staff to hire active managers assigned to outperform particular benchmarks. (We will discuss benchmarks in Session 7 on performance evaluation. For the moment, you can think of a manager benchmark simply as a market index.) To produce this outperformance, the managers must hold portfolios that differ in composition from their benchmarks. Of course, underlying the use of active managers is the assumption that the managers' investment processes can identify investment opportunities that will produce a positive excess return relative to their benchmarks.

An active manager's decisions will not always be correct; as a result, returns above and below the benchmark will be greater (perhaps much greater) than will those of a passive manager. Although the staff can give the manager instructions regarding how much volatility relative to the benchmark is acceptable, this risk is an unavoidable part of active management. Furthermore, the management fees of active managers are generally much higher than those of passive managers and represent a major hurdle that active managers must clear to keep up with passive managers' performance.

The use of active management in an asset class requires a series of beliefs on the investment committee's part. The trustees must believe that

- managers exist who can produce a positive excess return relative to an appropriate benchmark,
- the staff can identify these managers,
- the staff can hire these managers to manage the Fund's assets,
- the trustees have the risk tolerance to endure extended periods of time when the manager underperforms the benchmark, and
- the staff can structure a team of these managers to reach the Fund's investment objectives.

The decision to hire active managers in a particular asset class requires the trustees to answer "yes" to *all* of these belief statements. A "no" answer to any of the statements implies that the Fund should not engage in active management in that asset class. By implication then, passive management ought to be the default position where it is available. (Some asset classes, such as private equity, can be accessed only through active management.)

Regarding the last belief statement, Molly, note that we could have a team of value added active managers yet not achieve the investment objective of outperforming the asset class target. Such an outcome would occur if the aggregate performance of the active managers' benchmarks is different from the Fund's asset class target. For example, if the Fund's asset class target for U.S. equities is the Russell 3000 Index and if the staff has hired only one active manager and that manager's benchmark is the Russell 3000 Value Index, then the manager could outperform its benchmark but underperform the Fund's asset class target, the Russell 3000. (In Session 5 on investment risk tolerance, we referred to this mismatch between the managers' benchmarks and the asset class target as style bias.) The point is that the staff must ensure that the implementation of the investment program is consistent with the Fund's investment objectives and policy asset mix.

Separate Accounts and Commingled Funds

The investment committee must also determine in what types of accounts the Fund's assets will be managed: either in a *separately managed account* or a *commingled fund*. A separately managed account is legally owned by the Fund and managed solely in the Fund's interests. Typically, a bank trustee holds custody of the assets and implements purchase and sale directions from the investment manager. Both the bank and the manager maintain valuation and accounting records of the account, which serves as an important check and balance in the Fund's governance process. Furthermore, the flow of money into

- Does the staff have authority to hire and fire managers independent of the investment committee? If not, how are the trustees involved in those decisions?

- Does the staff use our consultant to help select managers? If so, is the Fund's consultant independent with respect to the managers it recommends?

- What considerations go into determining which types of alternative investments to own in the Fund?

- What return and risk expectations do we have for our alternative investments, and how do they compare to our publicly traded investments?

- What is the size of the commitment made to alternative investments that the Fund is obligated to invest but has not yet been called by the managers?

- How do we evaluate the potential introduction of a new asset class? What considerations should be involved? Do we have the expertise to select and monitor a new asset class?

- What if a potential new asset class is without a long history? How does that affect our analysis?

Session 7. Performance Evaluation

> He who would search for pearls must dive below.
>
> —*John Dryden*

How is the Fund performing? That's a simple (seemingly obvious) question, Molly, which undoubtedly you'll want to ask at your first investment committee meeting. That question is open to different interpretations, however, and as a result, you'll likely receive a wide variety of answers. Before you can make any sense out those answers, you'll want to familiarize yourself with some of the key concepts that underlie investment performance evaluation. The investment committee likes to phrase those concepts in the form of several questions:

- Why is performance evaluation important?
- How should performance be measured?
- How is performance assessed as either good or bad?
- What caused the observed performance?
- Is the performance the result of luck or skill?
- What should be done with all this performance information?

The Importance of Performance Evaluation

From the trustees' perspective, performance evaluation is important because it assists in exercising appropriate oversight of the investment program. It provides a regular assessment of how the Fund is performing relative to established investment objectives. When conducted properly, performance evaluation offers a valuable "quality control" check that describes not only the investment results of the Fund and its constituent parts relative to objectives but also explains the sources of that relative performance. The sources of investment performance can, and should, be directly linked to decisions relating to the Fund's investment policy and investment strategies.

Performance evaluation helps reinforce the hierarchy of accountability, responsibility, and authority in the Fund's governance structure. Investment managers have accountability, responsibility, and authority for investment decisions relating to the securities that they hold in their portfolios. Similarly, the Fund's staff, perhaps together with the Fund's consultant, has responsibility, accountability, and authority for decisions relating to the allocation to investment managers and asset classes. Ultimately, you and the other trustees have accountability, responsibility, and authority for the decisions relating to long-term performance of the entire investment program.

Performance evaluation enhances the effectiveness of the Fund's investment program by acting as a feedback-and-control mechanism. It identifies and focuses on the program's strengths and weaknesses. It assists in reaffirming a commitment to effective investment policies, strategies, processes, people, and organization. Similarly, it helps to direct attention to poorly performing operations. Moreover, performance evaluation provides a demonstration that a successful investment program is being conducted in an appropriate and effective manner.

Molly, you're busy with your "day job." You don't have time to familiarize yourself with every aspect of Freedonia University's investment decision making, so you may have difficulty in your trustee role assessing the effectiveness of the Fund's investment program. Properly presented, performance evaluation should help point you to the right questions regarding the investment program and assist you in taking corrective action when necessary.

Performance Measurement

At its most elementary level, performance evaluation requires measuring investment results, which leads to the question of what metric to use. A reasonable first response might be to focus on changes in the value of the Fund. Is there more or less money in the Fund at the end of the period than at the beginning? The investment committee certainly needs to pay close attention to the Fund's asset balance. Because the trustees have limited control over the timing and amount of contributions and withdrawals made to and from the Fund, however, the change in its value fails to provide an accurate indicator of how its investments are performing. The staff could be doing a superior job of investing the Fund's assets, but the value of the Fund could decline because of large withdrawals and a lack of recent contributions. Alternatively, the staff could be doing a poor job of investing the Fund's assets, but its value could increase because of a large contribution and a lack of withdrawals.

Because the change in the value of the Fund is not a good measure of investment performance, what alternative metric should be used? The investment community typically uses *rate of return* as the metric to measure investment performance. The rate of return calculates the percentage increase or decrease in the value of the Fund after removing the effect of various non-investment-related changes.

However, things are not quite that simple. There are different methods of calculating rates of return. During your investment committee meetings, you will hear mention of *time-weighted rate of return* (TWR) and *money-weighted rate of return* (MWR). We don't need to go into the math behind calculating these rates of return, but it would be helpful for you to understand why these different rates of return are used. The concise explanation is that the appropriate use of these methods depends on who controls the timing and size of money flows into and out of an investment account. Importantly, all of our return measures are stated after accounting for all fees and expenses incurred by the investment program.

The staff reports the TWR when the investment manager has little or no control over the flow of external funds into and out of the manager's account. It effectively measures the rate of return as if $1 were invested in the account. That $1 is deposited at the beginning of the period and left to grow or shrink according to the investment results alone, with no money subsequently put into or taken out of the account during the period. The calculation is based on the percentage change in the value of the account between the dates when contributions or withdrawals from the account have occurred. These periodic returns are then linked together to determine performance for longer periods of time. In most cases, the investment committee has delegated to the staff control of the amount of money and the time period over which the investment manager will manage the Fund's assets. Typically, when a manager is hired, the staff decides how much money to give the manager and when to make contributions and withdrawals. For various reasons, the staff may choose to withdraw money from or add money to the manager's investment authority. If so, the timing and amount of money flowing into and out of the manager's account should not affect the calculation of the rate of return. Hence, the TWR is the appropriate performance measure in this situation (as it also is in the case of measuring the performance of the entire fund).

Contrast these circumstances to an investment with a private equity manager. The staff makes a commitment to invest a certain amount of money with the manager over a particular period of time. When the manager identifies an attractive investment opportunity, the manager makes a call on the Fund for a portion of the money that the Fund has committed. In this case, the *manager* determines the timing and amount of the investment contribution. The manager also controls when and how the investment proceeds are returned to the Fund. Because the investment manager has control of contributions and withdrawals, the staff reports the MWR.

The staff calculates the MWR by computing the rate of return that will discount all the contributions and withdrawals (at the time of their occurrence) to equal the value (usually appraised or estimated) of the account at the end of the measurement period. In this case, unlike the TWR, the size and the timing of the cash flows will affect calculation of the rate of return.

Alternatively, we can think of the MWR as the average growth rate of all dollars invested in the Fund. If a contribution is made prior to a period of relatively strong investment results, that action will enhance the MWR. Conversely, investments made prior to a weak performance period will drag down the MWR. (The MWR is also known in finance textbooks as the "internal rate of return," or IRR.)

Performance Benchmarks

Once the rates of return for the managers' accounts, the asset classes, and the total fund are determined, attention naturally turns to whether those returns are good or bad. To assess the "goodness" of a rate of return, we need a standard or benchmark with which to compare the result. Although there may be many candidates for a benchmark, we believe that the most informative assessment of investment performance occurs when the benchmark has certain basic properties:

- *Unambiguous*—the benchmark should be clearly understood by all parties involved in the investment program.

- *Investable*—the benchmark should represent an investable alternative; that is, the trustees could choose to hold the benchmark rather than hire the particular manager.

- *Measurable*—the benchmark's rate of return should be readily calculable.

- *Appropriate*—the benchmark should reflect the manager's typical risk characteristics and area of expertise.

- *Specified in advance*—the benchmark must be specified prior to the evaluation period and known to all interested parties.

- *Owned*—the benchmark should be acknowledged and accepted as an appropriate accountability standard by the party responsible for the performance.

Benchmarks that possess these properties provide the investment committee with a fair standard to use in assessing an account's performance. Many organizations use published market indices (e.g., the S&P 500) as benchmarks for their individual managers. Those indices may satisfy the benchmark quality criteria, but not always. The staff works closely with the Fund's managers to develop acceptable benchmarks, which, in some cases, results in custom benchmarks designed specifically for a manager. At the asset class level, however— say, for the U.S. stock market—the staff is likely to use a published index. To evaluate the total fund, the staff uses a policy portfolio, which is a combination of the asset class targets, weighted by the policy allocations assigned to the asset classes. (In Session 2 on investment policy and Session 5 on investment risk tolerance, we call these policy allocations the "policy asset mix.") This policy portfolio represents the amount and type of investment risk that the investment committee believes will give the Fund the best chance of fulfilling its mission, meeting its investment objectives, and providing consistency with the trustees' collective risk tolerance.

You may wonder why we need benchmarks in the performance evaluation process. Why not simply compare how the investment program is doing relative to the Fund's peers? After all, businesses constantly "benchmark" their operations against those of their competitors. Indeed, peer group comparisons are quite popular in the investment community. Despite their seeming simplicity, however, they fail to contain a number of the properties required of a valid benchmark. For example, peer groups are rarely appropriate because they are likely to contain accounts that have different missions, investment objectives, and risk tolerances. Also, peer groups are neither investable nor specified in advance. What investment strategy within the peer group will deliver top-quartile performance? Our staff might be able to discern that strategy after the fact, but the staff does not know prior to the evaluation period which funds will be the most successful. As a result, peer groups represent "alternative decisions" that could never be selected. Moreover, they tend to be subject to "survivor bias" whereby the worst performing funds drop out of the index, artificially pushing up the reported returns of the peer group. Finally, peer groups are ambiguous. The staff has little knowledge of the constituents of the peer group. Therefore, comparisons say nothing about why the Fund performed better or worse than other funds. One would need a detailed understanding of the other funds' investment policies, objectives, and strategies to ascertain what factors produced those funds' results.

Because of these deficiencies, the investment committee has been careful about how it uses peer group comparisons. Generally, the trustees have requested that the staff emphasize comparisons with thoughtfully selected benchmarks designed to represent the risk tolerance and objectives embedded in the investment program.

Performance Attribution

Performance evaluation involves not only measuring performance by calculating a rate of return and assessing performance by comparing that rate of return with an appropriate benchmark, but it also entails identifying the factors that caused that relative performance. This process is known as "*performance attribution.*" Molly, you can think of performance attribution as an informed look at the past.

As a trustee, you would like to understand *why* the Fund's managers performed better or worse than their benchmarks or why the Fund in aggregate has produced its results. Identifying the factors that caused an investment result is an important first step.

Because many factors can explain a particular investment outcome, the investment committee finds it helpful to identify and attribute performance to those factors that are linked to the investment management process. That type of analysis provides the trustees with valuable feedback that will either reinforce the effectiveness of the management process or cause a rethinking of it. Essentially, the method by which performance is explained or attributed should directly relate to the management process by which investment decisions are made. This link will, in turn, provide valuable messages to the management process. These connections are depicted in **Figure 2**. The more relevant the performance attribution to the management process, the more likely that it will influence that process positively in the future.

Figure 2. Performance Attribution Feedback Loop

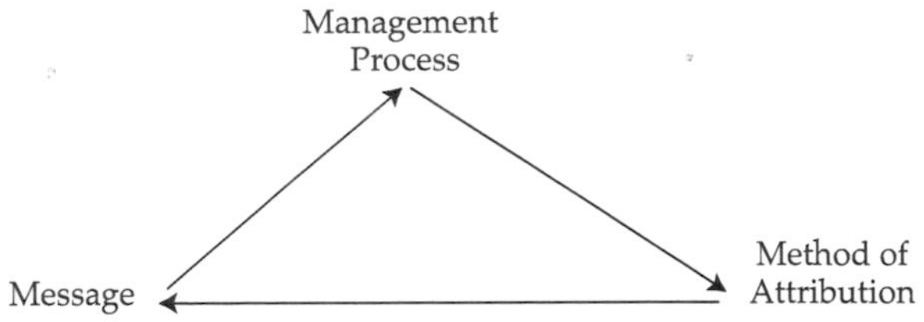

For example, the staff has retained an investment manager who assigns analysts to research companies in particular industries. The analysts, in turn, recommend companies to buy, sell, or hold based on their analyses. Portfolio managers use these recommendations, together with their own assessments of which industries are attractive and unattractive, to build their investment portfolios. An attribution method that identifies the contributions of the individual analysts and portfolio managers helps the trustees determine whether the manager's investment process is effective and whether we should continue to employ that manager. Performance attribution conducted at the level of the individual manager account is called "micro attribution."

Performance attribution at the asset class and total fund level is termed "macro attribution." The investment committee finds macro attribution particularly valuable because that analysis explains the impact of investment policy decisions on the Fund's success. At the total fund level, macro attribution allows the investment committee to examine the impact of important implementation decisions, including setting a policy asset mix, hiring managers, and allocating assets to the managers.

Dropping down one macro attribution level to the performance of an asset class relative to its asset class target, we find it depends on much more than how the underlying investment managers performed. The relative performance of an asset class investment is also the result of the staff's decisions about the allocation of assets to the individual managers within each class. It involves structuring and managing a team of managers.

The investment committee uses performance evaluation for purposes broader than simply accepting a numerical report submitted periodically. Instead, the attribution reports help to develop a dialogue with the staff about the primary elements that have driven investment results. The reports serve to highlight certain aspects of the investment program, and the trustees use that information to ask informed questions of the staff. You'll find the attribution reports to be one of your most useful tools in understanding the workings of Freedonia University's investment program.

Performance Appraisal

Investment management operates in an environment of uncertainty. Unforeseeable events drive investment returns. Because neither the staff nor the managers are omniscient in their investment decision making, the challenge of performance evaluation is to distinguish between luck and skill. We refer to that process as *"performance appraisal."*

You can think of investment skill as the ability to outperform an appropriate benchmark consistently over time. As mentioned in Session 5 on investment risk tolerance, we call returns relative to a benchmark "active management returns." All managers' returns (even the returns of passive managers) will tend to fluctuate around their benchmarks, generating positive relative performances in some periods and negative relative performances in others—the variability we consider active management risk. As we discussed, active managers will display more variability in their returns relative to their benchmarks than will passive managers. Importantly, superior active managers will tend to produce larger positive active management returns more frequently than will inferior active managers. Similarly, superior passive managers will tend to closely track the benchmark's return (that is, produce zero active management returns) more consistently than inferior passive managers.

To identify skillful managers, the staff compares the active management returns earned by the managers with their active management risk. Skillful managers will demonstrate higher active management returns per unit of active management risk that they take on. There are a number of risk-adjusted performance measures in common use. During your investment committee meetings, you will likely hear mention of two of the more popular measures—namely, the *Sharpe ratio* and the *information ratio*. Both weigh rewards earned per unit of risk taken. The Sharpe ratio compares an account's excess return (actual return less the risk-free return) with the total risk of the account, where risk is measured as the standard deviation of the account's returns. The information ratio is a variation of the Sharpe ratio. It compares an account's active management return (actual return less the benchmark return) with the active management risk of the account, where active management risk is measured as the standard deviation of the account's active management returns.

Because it is often difficult for the trustees to examine the details behind these risk-adjusted measures, the staff uses quality control charts as a presentation tool. An example is shown in **Figure 3**. The solid line in the middle is the manager's cumulative return over the entire evaluation period. In this case, it is a manager's cumulative active return (actual return less the benchmark return). The dotted lines are statistically derived confidence bands. When the return line is at or above the top dotted line, the performance has been exceptionally good. When it is at or below the bottom dotted line, the performance has been

Figure 3. Quality Control Chart: Cumulative Performance of Actual Portfolio vs. Benchmark

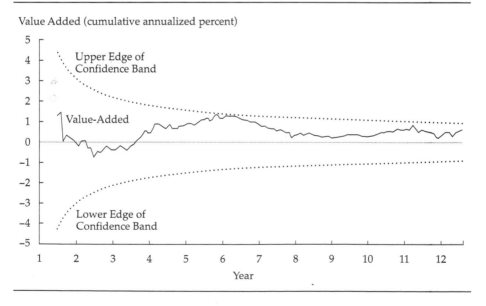

Value Added (cumulative annualized percent)

©2011 The Research Foundation of CFA Institute

exceptionally bad. It is difficult to draw conclusions about a manager's skill if the solid line consistently falls well within the dotted lines, other than that performance has been insignificantly positive or negative relative to the benchmark.

Putting It All Together

Trustees frequently feel a need to "do something": fire a manager, hire a manager, invest in a new strategy, or terminate an existing one. You didn't achieve your professional success by sitting on your hands, after all. Unfortunately, as a trustee, this attitude can be counterproductive. It often leads to "buy high, sell low" investment outcomes.

Trustees (and the staff) receive an overwhelming amount of performance data, all of it having to do with the past. Although nothing can be done about the past, a number of questions arise about applying all this information to future decisions: What can be learned from performance evaluation to help improve the management of the Fund? When should the investment committee revisit and rethink its policies? What changes or decisions should the trustees make? When should those actions be taken?

Relying solely on past performance to determine what to do is like driving a car by looking through the rearview mirror. As a trustee, Molly, to do something that will have a reasonable chance of improving future performance, you need to put past performance in proper perspective and then augment that knowledge with additional insights and information.

Even skillful managers and effective investment programs will have periods of unusually bad performance, possibly extending for multiyear periods. What should trustees and staff members do when risk-adjusted performance has been unusually bad? Relying solely on past performance, even when properly adjusted for risk, can be counterproductive. Negative returns relative to the benchmark cannot be ignored, of course, and should be discussed, but the review needs to be augmented with other information, much of it qualitative in nature. As a start, the investment staff finds it helpful to review the rationale and decision process that was used to implement the particular investment in the first place. Such a review involves asking what may have changed and what has been learned.

For example, when hiring or firing an investment manager, the staff conducts an assessment of a range of qualitative and quantitative management factors, including:

- *People*—experience, expertise, organizational structure.
- *Process*—philosophy, resources, decision making.
- *Procedures*—trading, quality control.
- *Price*—fees and expenses.
- *Performance*—discounted for risk, deflated by the benchmark, and net of fees.

Also, regardless of whether the investments are performing well or poorly, the staff regularly assesses investment strategy decisions relative to their economic rationale, diversification value, and liquidity characteristics.

The management of an investment fund is similar to piloting an aircraft. The pilot receives a tremendous amount of information about the location of the plane and current flying conditions. Once a course is set, however, there are typically few changes that should be made. Similarly, once the trustees have determined the Fund's investment objectives and how best to achieve them, the investment path is set. Although the journey may be a bit bumpy, the question you continually face is whether the Fund is "on course." There is no one right answer, but in general, keeping a focus on the Fund's planned route and making only modest midcourse corrections has served the Freedonia University investment program well in the past.

Takeaways

- Performance evaluation is important because it
    - informs trustees how the Fund is doing relative to its mission and objectives,
    - establishes a hierarchy of responsibility, authority, and accountability,
    - identifies the investment program's strengths and weaknesses,
    - reaffirms a commitment to successful policies and decisions,
    - focuses attention on poorly performing operations, and
    - provides evidence as to whether the investment program is being managed properly.
- Performance measurement is the process of calculating the rate of return of an account (i.e., a fund, an asset class, or a manager).
- Two measures of rate of return are common: time-weighted rate of return and money-weighted rate of return. Both should be reported after accounting for all investment-related fees and expenses.
- The TWR is unaffected by the timing of money flows into and out of a fund. The MWR is sensitive to those flows.
- The TWR is the appropriate return measure when the account manager has no control over money flows. When the account manager can determine when money comes into or goes out of an account, the MWR is the proper return measure.
- Assessing investment performance is done by comparing it with a benchmark that is unambiguous, investable, measurable, appropriate, specified in advance, and owned.

- Performance attribution involves crediting performance to factors that caused the actual outcome relative to the benchmark.

- Performance attribution at the level of the investment manager account is micro attribution; at the asset class and total fund level, it is macro attribution.

- Performance appraisal involves assessing the skill of an investment manager by examining the consistency of returns relative to the benchmark.

- Patience and a focus on investment policy can help avoid expensive and unproductive responses to near-term performance disappointments.

QUESTIONS MOLLY SHOULD ASK

- How do we calculate performance measurement for our individual managers, asset classes, and the Fund?

- Who is responsible for the Fund's performance measurement (i.e., the staff, the custodian bank, the consultant, or some other organization)?

- What are the benchmarks we use to evaluate our investment program? Are they fair and appropriate?

- Can you provide examples in the past when performance evaluation has identified particular strengths and weaknesses in our investment program, and what were our responses to those observations?

- How are we doing? Do our investment results indicate that we fulfilling our investment mission and objectives?

- What various performance measurement, attribution, and evaluation reports does the investment committee receive? How frequently are they produced? Can I see examples of past reports?

- Do we integrate performance evaluation information with decisions regarding investment policy? Asset classes? Investment managers? Investment risk?

- How do we evaluate investment performance for products with a short (or no) track record?

- If individual investment managers leave a firm and go to another firm or start a new firm, should we view their track records from their previous firms as portable?

- What standards do we use to evaluate asset classes with nonmarketable investments, such as private equity?

- What qualitative criteria do we use to evaluate investment managers?

- What role does the consultant play in interpreting performance attribution and evaluation reports for the staff and trustees?
- How do we evaluate the performance of the staff when we change asset allocations and require a large transition of assets from one class to another?
- How do we take into account the impact of unique market events when evaluating performance?

Session 8. Ethics in Investing

> Few things are harder to put up with than
> the annoyance of a good example.
>
> —*Mark Twain*

Molly, one of the important reasons the regents selected you to be a university investment trustee is that you have a strong record of integrity. Even the best-intentioned trustees, however, should be versed in the ethical standards appropriate for their role on the investment committee. Your ethical conduct reflects on not only the investment committee but also the university. In this session, we want to give you a brief overview of some considerations that you might bear in mind as you prepare to join the investment committee.

Recognized Principles of Trustee Ethical Conduct

You can access a number of publications that address ethics and standards of professional investment conduct. For example, CFA Institute has published a code of conduct for investment professionals as well as a code of conduct for trustees of pension and endowment funds. We encourage you to review them. The ethical principles recognized in these publications can be summarized as follows:

- Act in the best interest of the Fund's beneficiaries.
- Act with prudence, competence, independence, and objectivity.
- Adhere to the Fund's mission and all related legal requirements.
- Act in a transparent manner in all official activities.
- Maintain confidentiality with regard to the Fund sponsor, beneficiaries, and fund investments.

Several years ago, one of the investment committee members asked permission to attend a conference to increase his understanding of investment issues. That request seemed to be reasonable, and the trustee's expenses were paid out of the Fund's assets. However, the trustee continued to attend conferences, almost every quarter, some of which were halfway around the world. The associated expenses were not insignificant, and other trustees began to wonder if this trustee was "acting in the best interest of the Fund's beneficiaries" or in the best interest of the trustee. Although the individual is no longer an investment trustee at Freedonia—and for that, the committee heaved a sigh of relief— in one sense, he performed a valuable service. He made questions of ethical conduct and *conflict of interest* a reality for the rest of the trustees and increased their dedication to establishing and practicing strong ethical standards.

"Shades of Gray": Recognizing and Resolving Ethical Dilemmas

Unfortunately, Molly, not all ethical questions are black or white. At times, the difference between acceptable and unacceptable ethical conduct is obvious, as in the case of the trustee and his conferences. At other times, it is a matter of "shades of gray," which makes it difficult to determine where to draw the line. Such cases will require your good judgment and solid ethical standards.

For example, a few years ago the Fund's CIO traveled to Edinburgh, Scotland, to visit one of the Fund's international equity managers. The manager's investment portfolio had experienced disappointing performance. While in Edinburgh, the CIO visited the investment manager's office, met with the various members of our investment management team there, and discussed the manager's investment strategy, rationale, and process. Subsequently, the CIO spent the weekend with the investment manager, playing golf and having dinner with the portfolio manager's wife and family. (The CIO paid for all of his own expenses.) Upon returning, the CIO recommended that we continue to retain the investment manager.

To some observers, the CIO's weekend activities appeared to be a conflict of interest or at least to make it difficult for him to form an objective opinion. In discussing the matter with the trustees, however, the CIO explained that he learned much more about the manager during the weekend than during the office visit. In particular, the CIO felt it was important to gain a better understanding of the manager's character, integrity, and attitude toward risk and return. And he felt he gained these additional insights by observing how the manager conducted himself outside the office (for example, in his relationship with his family, how he played the game of golf—particularly, the risks and rewards he incurred and his honesty in playing the game). The trustees accepted the CIO's rationale, primarily because they appreciate the importance of qualitative information in assessing an investment manager.

Establishing Ethical Conduct Guidelines

The trustees revisit the issue of ethical practices periodically. Their approach has been to (1) encourage a discussion and identification of ethical issues and dilemmas, (2) solicit input and recommendations from various sources, and (3) adopt guidelines specific to the situations under consideration. Interestingly, one of your trustee colleagues has said that she asks herself how the investment committee's reputation would be affected if our university's student newspaper published (in a fair and balanced manner) a particular guideline and the trustees' underlying rationale for adopting it. If the investment committee's reputation, at a minimum, would not be harmed and, better yet, might even be enhanced, she views the guideline as appropriate.

The investment committee's ethical guidelines change over time because of the need for flexibility. Issues surface that must be addressed. What never changes are the core ethical principles upon which the guidelines are based. Those principles are incorporated in a Freedonia University Code of Ethical Conduct, and the guidelines serve to focus more specifically on the investment program's particular circumstances. As a rule, the more thorough the documentation of procedures and policy is, the less likely the trustees are to encounter ethical conduct concerns.

In general, most of the ethical issues that the trustees wrestle with involve either the expenditure of the Fund's assets (other than for beneficiary payments) or relationships with the organizations with which the staff and trustees do business. The investment committee has direct responsibility, authority, and accountability for the ethical conduct of individual trustees and the staff. That situation is not the same, however, for the external organizations providing services to the Fund. Although the trustees have responsibility for the ethical conduct of these organizations, the investment committee has only limited authority over their actions. Accordingly, the trustees seek assurance that these organizations are conducting their business activities in a manner consistent with the investment committee's ethical principles. The trustees require that these organizations—primarily, our investment managers, consultant, and bank custodian—provide the staff with their own codes of ethical conduct. The staff reviews these documents, assures the trustees that the ethical policies are acceptable, and monitors the organizations to ensure that the organizations' conduct is consistent with their codes.

The investment committee's interest in ethical conduct goes beyond a mere concern about its reputation and that of the university. The trustees sincerely believe that positive ethical conduct is a necessary condition for a well-managed fund; without it, the investment program is unlikely to produce results consistent with the Fund's mission and investment objectives.

Achievement of a commitment to ethical conduct depends largely on the interest and integrity of the individual trustees, which comes back to where we started. We are delighted to have a trustee like you: a person with high integrity, moral values, good judgment, and a serious commitment to making a positive contribution to the Fund.

Welcome aboard, Molly.

Takeaways

- A number of publications address ethics and standards of professional investment conduct. In particular, CFA Institute has published a code of conduct for investment professionals and a code of conduct for trustees of pension and endowment funds.
- The following ethical principles are appropriate for trustees to focus on:
  - acting in the best interest of the Fund's beneficiaries,
  - acting with prudence, competence, independence, and objectivity,
  - adhering to the Fund's mission and all related legal requirements,
  - requiring transparency of all involved parties, and
  - maintaining confidentiality with regard to the fund sponsor, beneficiaries, and fund investments.
- Ethical guidelines can help provide additional clarity to specific situations and circumstances.
- In addition to maintaining an ethical code of conduct and guidelines for individual trustees and the staff, it is important to assess the ethical conduct of organizations with which the fund has a relationship.
- The best assurance of ethical investment conduct is the integrity, principles, and moral values of trustees and staff members.

QUESTIONS MOLLY SHOULD ASK

- May I have a copy of the CFA Institute codes of conduct and also a list of other publications dealing with ethical conduct for trustees?
- May I have a copy of any principles and guidelines that we have adopted as a code of conduct?
- Does the staff have a similar code of conduct? How does that code differ from the one that applies to the trustees?
- Do the trustees sign a statement that lists any potential conflicts of interest that they may have in carrying out their duties?
- Have there been serious ethical issues in the past involving trustees other than the one you described? If so, what were those issues and how were they resolved?
- Is there a facility for staff members to report confidentially any ethical problems that they observe or experience?
- Is it viewed as a conflict of interest for a trustee to discuss positive and negative experiences that he or she may have observed as a trustee of another fund?
- Should a trustee suggest a manager for potential hiring if the trustee has a business relationship (now or in the past) with that manager?
- What guidelines do we have regarding items of value that can be accepted from an outside organization?

Appendix A. Freedonia University Endowment Fund Governance Policy Statement

The purpose of a governance policy is to delineate clearly the delegation of authority, accountability, and responsibility of the investment committee and investment staff in the policies and operation of the fund's investment program. Governance policy focuses on those organizational design elements critical to effective decision making. Effective decision making can be achieved only in an environment of mutual trust and respect, in which decisions are made and implemented quickly and lines of authority and responsibility are clear to all.

The Freedonia University Board of Regents has delegated to the Freedonia University Investment Committee (the Committee) the authority and responsibility for management and oversight of the Freedonia University Endowment Fund's assets (the Fund). The Committee recognizes that there are different types of fiduciary roles in the management and oversight of the Fund. The Committee is the governing fiduciary with the ultimate responsibility for the investment program. The chief investment officer (CIO) and his/her investment staff are the managing fiduciaries of the investment program, charged with the day-to-day management responsibility for the Fund. The investment program also includes several operating fiduciaries, such as outside investment managers, who are given the authority to make decisions, albeit with respect to only a portion of the Fund assets and within the scope of approved mandates.

In general, the Committee's responsibilities are focused on expressing the Fund's mission and choosing the investment policies most likely to achieve it. The Committee is also responsible for monitoring staff effectiveness and seeing that its policies are properly implemented by the managing and operating fiduciaries to which it has delegated specific authorities. The Committee

- defines the Fund's mission,
- establishes performance goals and investment objectives for the Fund and monitors actual performance versus these goals and objectives,
- establishes the policy asset mix and acceptable asset allocation ranges around that policy asset mix,

- approves asset allocation deviations from outside approved ranges,
- determines the acceptable level of active management risk,
- determines acceptable asset classes and subcategories (e.g., emerging markets, absolute return strategies),
- approves asset class targets,
- approves the investment staff's annual operating budget,
- reviews governance procedures and makes recommendations to the Board of Regents,
- approves custodian bank and audit relationships,
- approves securities lending arrangements,
- evaluates and retains the CIO,
- ensures resources adequate to perform the Fund's mission effectively, and
- provides information and recommendations to the Board of Regents as required.

The Committee recognizes that its professional investment staff is best situated to make day-to-day investment decisions. The Committee has delegated authority to the CIO to implement key policy and operational decisions for the Fund. The CIO

- evaluates, retains, and terminates investment managers,
- determines asset allocation deviations within approved ranges,
- evaluates, retains, and terminates consultants and other service providers,
- acquires sufficient internal staff and resources to meet objectives and fiduciary responsibilities,
- establishes performance benchmarks and investment guidelines for individual investment managers,
- establishes and implements manager-monitoring procedures,
- determines asset class and manager-rebalancing strategy,
- provides liquidity for payments to beneficiaries and to fund operations,
- provides recommendations to the Committee as needed to aid in the decision-making process,
- provides the Committee with adequate information and resources to make policy decisions and monitor fund performance, and
- provides the Committee with analytical data regarding cost-effectiveness issues.

Appendix B. Freedonia University Pension Fund Investment Policy Statement

The Fund's Mission

The mission statement defines the purposes for which the pension fund exists as a financial entity. Typically, a pension fund will have multiple missions, and those missions will be assigned different priorities. In total, these missions provide the framework around which detailed elements of the fund's investment policy are established.

The mission of the Freedonia University (the University) pension fund (the Fund) is to secure and protect the retirement benefits promised to the employees who participate in the University's defined-benefit pension plan (the Plan). All University employees meeting minimum age and service requirements are eligible for a pension benefit. The University finances the Plan's benefits through both periodic contributions and the investment earnings on assets held in the Fund. The Freedonia University Investment Committee (the Committee) recognizes that a sound investment program implemented through the Fund is essential to the University's ability to meet its pension promise.

The excess of the Fund's assets relative to the Plan's liabilities (the Plan Surplus) provides crucial security for the employees' retirement benefits. Therefore, the Fund's primary mission is to accumulate and maintain a sufficiently positive Plan Surplus to protect and sustain currently promised benefits.

The Committee acknowledges the material impact that funding the pension promise has on the University's financial performance. To enable the University to continue offering secure pension benefits to plan participants, the Committee believes that the Fund should pursue the following secondary missions:

1. Minimize the present value of the contributions that the University must make to the Plan over the long term.

2. Avoid both substantial volatility in cash contributions and sizable fluctuations in the Plan Surplus.

These two secondary Fund missions affect the Fund's investment strategies and often represent conflicting goals. That is, minimizing long-run funding costs implies an aggressive investment program whereas dampening the volatility of contributions and avoiding large fluctuations in the Plan Surplus imply a conservative set of investments. The Committee places greater emphasis on the strategy of reducing the present value of contributions made to the Fund, as it is most consistent with the University's long-run goal of conserving money to apply to other important University projects.

Risk Tolerance

Risk tolerance refers to the investment committee's willingness to bear adverse outcomes in pursuit of the pension fund's missions. It indicates the trade-off that the committee will accept between, on the one hand, the likelihood and costs of failing to achieve the goals set out for the pension fund and, on the other hand, the likelihood and rewards derived from exceeding those goals.

The Committee's risk tolerance with respect to the primary aspect of the Fund's mission is extremely low. The Committee is unwilling to undertake investment strategies that might jeopardize the ability of the Fund to finance the pension benefits promised to plan participants.

However, funding the pension promise in an economical manner is critical to the University's ability to continue to provide pension benefits to plan participants. Thus, the Committee actively seeks to lower the cost of funding the Plan's pension promise by taking on types of risk for which it expects to be compensated over the long run. The Committee understands that an aggressive investment approach to risk taking can result in periods of disappointing performance for the Fund in which the Plan Surplus may decline. These periods, in turn, can temporarily lead to higher required contributions. Nevertheless, the Committee believes that such an approach, prudently implemented, best serves the long-run interests of the University and, therefore, of plan participants.

Investment Objectives

A pension fund's investment objectives identify the set of portfolio management results that the investment committee believes would signal a successful investment program. Unlike the broad goals described in the fund's mission statement, investment objectives are specific, quantifiable investment results expected to be achieved over specific time intervals. Those investment objectives should be: unambiguous and measurable, specified in advance, actionable and attainable, and consistent with the fund's mission and should reflect the committee's risk tolerance.

The Committee's investment objectives are expressed in terms of reward and risk expectations relative to investable benchmarks. The Committee specifies investment objectives at three investment management levels: (1) total fund, (2) asset classes, and (3) individual investment managers. At each level, benchmarks have been established that represent the returns and risks that could be achieved through passive management. Performance at all levels of the investment program is always expressed net of all fees and expenses. Performance of the benchmarks is reported without deducting the costs of passive management. As a result, active management can add value to the investment program by at least matching the benchmark's performance.

At the total fund level, the Committee expects that its investment program will at least match (net of fees and expenses) the returns produced by a combination of the asset class targets over a minimum evaluation period of five years. The weights used to compute that combination represent the asset classes' respective policy asset mix allocations. The Committee expects that total fund returns will be produced without assuming more capital market risk than is implied by the Fund's policy asset mix.

At the asset class level, the Committee expects that its investments in each asset class will at least match the performance of the respective asset class target over the five-year evaluation period. Because of the mix of manager styles within each asset class, the Committee understands that individual manager returns relative to those of the asset class target may vary considerably over time. Therefore, the Committee focuses on the aggregate performance of the investment managers relative to the asset class target. Furthermore, the Committee recognizes that, because of the uncertain nature of active management, even the aggregate of the investment managers' returns may fall below the returns of the asset class target for extended periods.

At the individual manager level, the Committee expects that each of its investment managers will at least match the performance of the manager's assigned benchmark over a five-year evaluation period. The Committee insists that the investment managers follow investment styles similar to their benchmarks and maintain active management risk within agreed-upon bounds.

Policy Asset Mix

A pension fund's policy asset mix is its long-run allocation to broadly defined classes of investable assets. Decisions about the policy asset mix are based on expectations regarding the fundamental rewards and risks offered by the capital markets. The policy asset mix must be consistent with the fund's mission statement and the risk tolerance of the investment committee. The policy asset mix is a significant determinant of the fund's future performance. There is no one right policy for all pension plans. Differences in missions, risk tolerances, and the financial strength of the sponsoring organizations—all these factors affect the asset mix decision.

For purposes of asset allocation, the Committee considers both traditional and alternative asset classes and strategies. Traditional asset classes include publicly traded stocks and bonds, traded both in U.S. and non-U.S. markets. Alternative investments are all other investments and comprise a range of nontraditional, privately held assets, including but not limited to the following: private equity, real estate, natural resource investments, high-yield debt, distressed securities, and absolute return strategies.

In general, the Committee takes a strategic approach to the policy asset mix decision. To determine the impact of various asset allocation alternatives, the Committee reviews a formal asset allocation study using both qualitative and quantitative inputs. The purpose of this study is to help the Committee evaluate the risk–return trade-offs of various asset mix policies. The qualitative factors include peer practices and staff expertise. After consideration of all the inputs and a discussion of its own collective risk tolerance, the Committee approves the appropriate policy asset mix for the Fund. The current policy asset mix is detailed in **Table B.1**.

Table B.1.

Asset Class	Long-Term Policy Weight (%)	Rebalancing Range (%)
U.S. equity	30	25–35
Non-U.S. developed-market equity	20	15–25
Emerging-market equity	10	5–15
U.S. fixed income	20	15–25
U.S. inflation-linked bonds	10	5–15
U.S. real estate	5	0–10
Alternative investments	5	0–10
Cash	0	0–5
Total	100	

The Committee believes that the substantial equity allocation and the diversified composition of the Fund's policy asset mix are consistent with the Fund's primary mission of securing the University's pension promise. Moreover, the Committee believes that the Fund's policy asset mix permits the pension fund to appropriately balance its secondary missions of minimizing the present value of future contributions as well as avoiding extreme volatility in contributions and large fluctuations in the Plan Surplus.

Rebalancing the Policy Asset Mix

The Committee has established a policy of maintaining the Fund at its policy asset mix over time. To the extent that the Fund's actual asset allocation deviates from the currently specified ranges, assets will be redistributed to achieve the desired allocation. This may be accomplished by reallocating among the Fund's investment managers, through a synthetic approach using financial futures, or by a combination of both. The Committee has authorized the use of financial futures to overlay the assets of the Fund to bring about a more exact match with target allocations. The use of financial futures avoids frequent adjustments to the investment managers' portfolios that are not economically justifiable.

Nonmarketable investments, such as private equity, are not included in the Fund's procedures for rebalancing back to the policy asset mix because of the illiquid nature of these investments and the fact that capital flows into and out of these investments are uncontrollable. The Committee endeavors to maintain the allocations to nonmarketable investments near their policy weights but recognizes that deviations may occur from time to time because of the uneven nature of capital drawdowns and distributions.

Asset Class Targets

An asset class target is a benchmark that characterizes the scope and nature of available investments within a whole asset class. In general, asset class targets are capitalization-weighted indices representing a significant percentage of the invest-able universe of securities in a particular asset class. For example, the S&P 500 Index is commonly used as the asset class target for U.S. common stocks. Asset class targets are important yardsticks for evaluating investment performance and for managing the style risk of programs that use multiple-specialist active investment managers.

The Committee has selected asset class targets for all of its publicly traded investment portfolios. The current targets are specified in **Table B.2**.

The Committee has not chosen asset class targets for the Fund's nonmarketable investments, which include private equity, real estate, and natural resources. The illiquidity of those investments and the lack of market pricing have hampered the development of widely accepted market indices for any of the types of nonmarketable investments that the Fund holds.

Table B.2.

Asset Class	Asset Class Target
U.S. equity	Russell 3000 Index
Non-U.S. developed-market equity	MSCI World ex US Index
Emerging-market equity	MSCI Emerging Markets Index
U.S. fixed income	Barclays Capital Aggregate Bond Index
U.S. inflation-linked bonds (TIPS[a])	Barclays Capital U.S. TIPS Index
U.S. real estate	NCREIF Property Index
Alternative investments	NA
Cash	90-day T-bills

NA = not applicable.
[a]Treasury Inflation-Protected Securities.

Investment Manager Structure

Investment manager structure refers to two aspects of investment policy within asset classes. First, the investment committee must determine the role that active management will play in its investment program. Second, to the extent that the investment committee uses active management, it must allocate funds among the managers hired to invest the pension fund's assets. In that respect, the investment committee must develop policies designed to control the amount of "style bias" and active management risk in the investment program.

As a general philosophy, the Committee endorses the use of active management to enhance the returns generated by the Fund's policy asset mix. The Committee recognizes the highly competitive nature of the capital markets and the corresponding fact that active management cannot be guaranteed to add value to the Fund's investment program. Nevertheless, the Committee believes that the potential rewards from active management are sufficiently large to justify the search for superior investment organizations.

The Committee has chosen to invest the Fund's actively managed assets with outside investment managers. Presently, the Committee does not view the investment in people required to adequately staff an internal money management operation as cost-effective. The Committee has provided the chief investment officer with the authority to make active investment decisions on a limited and opportunistic basis.

With respect to active strategies, the Committee believes that *people* and *process* are at the very heart of a sustainable competitive advantage in the business of investment management. The Committee prefers to retain only those investment managers with experienced people and tested processes whose interests are aligned with those of the Fund. In terms of strategy, the Committee prefers to retain specialist investment managers who focus their efforts on selecting securities within asset classes and pursue well-defined investment approaches based on fundamental principles of security valuation.

Except in nonmarketable asset classes, each manager is required to designate or make available an appropriate benchmark. The manager's benchmark will be evaluated relative to six basic criteria:

- *Unambiguous*—the names and weights of securities comprising the benchmark are clearly delineated.
- *Investable*—the option is available to forgo active management and simply hold the benchmark.
- *Measurable*—the benchmark's return can be readily calculated on a reasonably frequent basis.
- *Appropriate*—the benchmark is consistent with the manager's investment style.

- *Specified in advance*—the benchmark is constructed prior to the start of an evaluation period.
- *Owned*—the manager accepts accountability for the composition and performance of the benchmark.

A manager's benchmark is used both to evaluate the manager's capabilities to add value and to characterize the manager's investment style for purposes of clarity and efficient structuring of investment managers within the asset class.

Within an asset class, assets are allocated to investment managers so that the total risk of the combined manager group relative to the asset class target is maintained within acceptable bounds. In particular, the Committee desires to cost-effectively minimize the risk posed by unintended deviations in the aggregate investment style of the investment managers from that of the asset class target (that is, style bias). The Committee allows for aggregate style deviations from the asset class target as a potential source of added value (e.g., tilting toward *value stocks*). However, the long-term source of added value is expected to derive from the active decisions of the investment managers. Therefore, the level of risk (return) from style management is targeted below the level of risk (return) expected to result from the aggregate effects of the investment managers' active strategies.

Performance Evaluation

Performance evaluation refers to the process of measuring and interpreting the performance of the investment program. It provides valuable information concerning the investment program's strengths and weaknesses and identifies areas of potentially profitable enhancements. Performance evaluation acts as a feedback-and-control mechanism carried out in the context of investment policy.

The Committee advocates a comprehensive approach to performance evaluation. The Committee regularly collects and reviews pertinent performance information regarding its investment program. At the total fund level, changes in the value of the Fund are broken down into specific key policy decisions. The Committee then examines how those decisions contributed to or detracted from the Fund's investment results. Through this process, the Committee seeks confirmation that its investment program is being carried out according to plan.

On the individual manager level, the Committee has approved an evaluation process implemented by the investment staff that specifies key qualitative and quantitative evaluation criteria and procedures for applying those criteria. As part of its ongoing manager review, the staff considers various indicators of the stability and effectiveness of its investment managers. If serious concerns arise from these reviews, the staff conducts examinations of investment managers and makes determinations as to their continued viability as part of the Fund's investment program.

Additional Investment Policy Issues

Investment Policy Review. The Committee may review elements of its investment policy from time to time. These reviews serve primarily to formally incorporate into the policy any enhancements and additions made to the Fund's investment program. The Committee views its investment policy as a robust set of guidelines and procedures and, therefore, does not anticipate major revisions unless the financial conditions of the Fund or the University change significantly.

Investment Guidelines. The Committee requires that investment guidelines be maintained for all of the Fund's investment managers who hold publicly traded securities. At a minimum, an investment manager's investment guidelines include specifications, mutually agreed to by the manager and the investment staff, related to the following:

- return and risk objectives,
- benchmark portfolio,
- authorized investments,
- portfolio composition constraints, and
- various investment and administrative practices.

The investment staff reviews manager guidelines on an ongoing basis to ensure compatibility and consistency with investment goals and objectives.

Proxy Voting. The Committee views the voting of proxies as an integral part of the investment decision-making process. Therefore, the Committee delegates the voting of all proxies to its investment managers.

Securities Lending and Swap and Other Derivative Transactions. The Committee believes that securities lending and swap and other derivative transactions that are conducted under appropriate guidelines offer attractive incremental returns for the Fund relative to the risk incurred. The Committee has authorized the chief investment officer (CIO) to engage in securities lending arrangements and swap and other derivative transactions with respect for all or some portion of the securities held by the Fund. Such authorization covers, without limitation, rate swap transactions, equity or equity index swaps, credit default swaps, repurchase transactions, or any other similar transactions recurrently entered into in the financial markets, any of which transactions may comprise a forward contract, swap, future, option, or other derivative on or with respect to one or more rates, currencies, commodities, equity securities, debt securities, economic indices, or other measures of economic risk or value.

Reporting. Since the Committee has delegated authority to the CIO to implement key policy and operational decisions for the Fund, the CIO shall provide the Committee with periodic reports that inform the Committee about the investment decisions made by the staff. On a quarterly basis, the CIO will provide a report to the Committee that highlights the changes to the investment portfolio with respect to investment managers. The report will identify the firm(s), strategy(ies), assets managed, and a brief rationale underlying the decision(s). On an annual basis, the CIO will provide the Committee with a complete listing of the Fund's investment managers, the format of which will include the manager's categorization, a brief strategy description, assets managed, and investment performance relative to appropriate benchmarks.

Glossary of Investment Terms

Absolute Return Fund: see Hedge Fund.

Active Management: a form of investment management that involves buying and selling financial assets with the objective of earning returns greater than a specified benchmark.

Active Management Return: the difference between a portfolio's return and the benchmark's return.

Active Management Risk: the risk taken by an active portfolio manager to earn active management returns by taking positions different from the benchmark; typically measured by the standard deviation of active management returns.

Actuary: a person or firm that specializes in estimating the liabilities associated with a benefit plan or an insurance trust.

Agency Conflict: the potential for conflict of interest between an agent and the person or organization for whom the agent is acting.

Alternative Investment: a term used to categorize assets other than traditional publicly traded stocks and bonds, including but not limited to private equity, real estate, hedge funds, commodities, timber, and infrastructure.

Asset Allocation: the process of determining the desired division of an investor's portfolio among available asset classes.

Asset Class: a broadly defined generic group of financial assets, such as stocks or bonds.

Benchmark: a portfolio with which the investment performance of an investor can be compared for the purpose of determining investment skill. A benchmark portfolio represents a relevant and investable alternative to the investor's actual portfolio and, in particular, is similar in terms of risk exposure.

Benefits: periodic payments promised or expected to be made to the designated beneficiaries of a pool of assets.

Benefit Security Ratio: see Funded Ratio.

Bond (also Fixed-Income Security): a type of investment in which the holder lends money to another entity and is then entitled to periodic payments of interest and a return of the capital at a specified time in the future.

Buyout: a form of private equity in which a partnership buys all the shares of a public company, usually taking on a large debt, to operate the company privately with the intention of eventually making a profit by taking the company public again or selling part or all of it to another business.

Commingled Fund: an investment vehicle that sells units of ownership in itself to one or more investors and uses the proceeds to purchase financial assets for the benefit of the investors. The investors have a *pro rata* claim on the assets of the fund proportional to their unit ownership.

Common Stock (also Equity; Stock): legal representations of an ownership position in a corporation.

Commodity: a physical (real) asset used as an input to a production process. Many commodities are traded in cash (spot) markets or on organized exchanges in the form of futures contracts.

Conflict of Interest: a situation in which a person who has a duty to one party acts in such a way as to benefit the person (or a related party) at the expense of the party to whom the duty is owed.

Contributions: money added to a pool of assets for the purpose of investment and, eventually, payment of benefits.

Correlation: a statistical measure of the covariation of two random variables (i.e., how much two variables change together).

Custodian Bank: a type of bank that provides safekeeping of financial securities for an investor, including the related accounting and reporting services.

Defined-Benefit Plan: a retirement plan in which the participants are promised a fixed benefit. The sponsoring organization takes the risk that its investments will be sufficient to provide these benefits.

Defined-Contribution Plan: a retirement plan in which a participant (and perhaps a sponsoring organization) makes fixed contributions and the participant bears the risk that the assets will be sufficient to provide adequate benefits upon retirement.

Diversification: the process of investing in more than one type of asset to reduce the risk of the entire portfolio.

Endowment: a gift, usually to an educational institution, whose purpose is to provide funding for a particular mission in perpetuity. Collectively, an aggregate of such gifts being managed in a single strategy.

Equity: see Common Stock.

Expected Return: the return on a security (or portfolio) that an investor anticipates receiving over a given time horizon.

Fiduciary: a person or entity that assumes responsibility to manage or oversee a pool of assets on behalf of some other person or entity, such as a pension fund or endowment. The fiduciary has a duty to act solely for the benefit of that entity (not himself/herself or some other entity).

Fiduciary Duty: a legal or ethical relationship of confidence or trust between two or more parties.

Financial Asset (also Security): a legal representation of the right to receive prospective future benefits under stated conditions.

Fixed-Income Security: see Bond.

Foundation: an entity that has some public mission (e.g., to cure a given disease) and provides grants to other entities to further that mission (e.g., by conducting scientific research to find a cure). It owns a pool of assets that are invested to provide income to fund that mission.

Funded Ratio (also Benefit Security Ratio): the ratio of the value of a fund's assets to the value of the fund's liabilities.

General Partner: an individual or firm that sources and obtains financing for the purchase of an asset and then manages that asset on behalf of other providers of capital (the limited partners).

Governance Structure: the set of processes by which a fund is managed for the benefit of some group of beneficiaries.

Growth Stocks: a segment of an equity market characterized by the stocks of companies that have experienced or are expected to experience earnings per share growth higher than the market as a whole. They also tend to display high price-to-earnings ratios relative to the market. Also called "glamour stocks."

Hedge Fund: a form of active management distinguished by a lack of traditional guidelines or benchmarks; a hedge fund typically uses derivatives, leverage, and/or short selling. The term is often synonymous with absolute return fund.

Indexing: see Passive Management.

Information Ratio: a risk-adjusted measure of portfolio active management performance. Mathematically, over an evaluation period, it is the annualized ratio of active management return to active management risk, where risk is measured by the standard deviation of the portfolio's active management returns.

Investable Universe: the aggregate of securities that is appropriate and available for selection under a particular investment mandate.

Investment Committee: a group of individuals who are responsible for determining the investment policy of a fund.

Investment Consultant: a professional (usually associated with a firm) who offers advisory services to a fund, most often in the areas of asset allocation, investment policy, and manager selection.

Investment Manager: a person or entity that creates and manages portfolios of securities for clients with money to invest.

Investment Policy: a component of the investment process that involves determining a fund's mission, objectives, and attitude toward the trade-off between expected return and risk.

Investment Policy Statement: a formal written document describing a fund's investment policy.

Investment Return: the percentage change in the value of an investment in a financial asset (or portfolio of financial assets) over a specified time period.

Investment Risk: the potential for loss accepted by an investor in the pursuit of investment return; alternatively, the uncertainty associated with the end-of-period value of an investment.

Investment Skill: the ability of an active manager to select portfolios that consistently have average returns greater than a given performance benchmark.

Liability: the present value of the accrued benefits promised to the beneficiaries of a fund.

Limited Partner: an individual or entity that provides equity financing to a general partner for the purchase of an investment but does not participate in the ongoing management of the investment.

Liquidity: property of a security that allows investors to convert the security to cash at a price similar to the price of the previous trade in the security (assuming that no significant new information has arrived since the previous trade).

Mandate: the strategy or performance benchmark used by an investment manager on behalf of and at the direction of a client.

Market Capitalization: the aggregate market value of a security, equal to the market price per unit of the security multiplied by the total number of outstanding units of the security.

Market Cycle: a period of time over which a particular security market moves from one peak to another or one trough to another.

Market Index: a collection of securities whose values are averaged to reflect the overall investment performance of a particular market for financial assets.

Money-Weighted Rate of Return: the rate of return on a portfolio over a particular period of time. It is the discount rate that makes the present value of cash flows into and out of the portfolio, as well as the portfolio's ending value, equal to the portfolio's beginning value.

Mutual Fund: a managed investment company, with an unlimited life, that stands ready at all times to purchase its shares from its owners and usually will continuously offer new shares to the public.

Overfunded: the status of a fund whose assets are greater in value than the associated plan's liabilities.

Passive Management (also Indexing): the process of buying and holding a well-diversified portfolio designed to produce substantially the same returns as a specified market index.

Peer Group: a set of investors (funds or managers) whose returns are used for a comparison with those of a given fund to determine how the given fund ranks among similar funds.

Performance Appraisal: the part of the performance evaluation process that attempts to determine whether the investment returns over an evaluation period have been achieved by skill or luck.

Performance Attribution: the part of the performance evaluation process that identifies sources of returns for a portfolio relative to a designated benchmark over an evaluation period.

Performance Evaluation: a component of the investment process involving periodic analysis of how a portfolio performed in terms of both returns earned and risks incurred.

Performance Measurement: the part of the performance evaluation process that calculates a portfolio's rate of return over an evaluation period.

Plan Participant: a member of a defined-benefit or defined-contribution plan to whom benefits are promised or are being paid.

Policy Asset Mix: a set of asset classes and desired percentage allocations to each such that the total portfolio displays the investor's desired risk and expected return profile; also referred to as the "policy portfolio," "policy benchmark," "policy asset allocation," or "strategic asset allocation."

Private Equity: a broad asset class generally involving buyouts, venture capital, and distressed debt converted to equity.

Real Estate: an investment in land and physical structures intended to provide a stream of rental or lease income and possibly capital appreciation.

Rebalancing: the process of buying and selling assets to restore a fund to its policy asset mix after market movements or net cash flows have changed the actual market weights of the various asset classes.

Relative Performance: the difference between a portfolio's return and the benchmark's return.

Risk Budgeting: a risk management technique in which assets are allocated efficiently so that the expected return of each asset is proportional to its contribution to portfolio risk.

Risk Management: a part of the investment process in which the risks of a portfolio are identified and quantified; then, strategies are developed to control those risks.

Risk Tolerance: the trade-off between risk and expected return demanded by a particular investor.

Scenario Analysis: a process whereby, for the purpose of designing appropriate investment strategies, an investor considers a number of possible future economic investment environments and the likelihood of those environments occurring.

Security: see Financial Asset.

Separately Managed Account: an investment vehicle that takes in funds from a single investor and uses the proceeds to purchase financial assets for the sole benefit of that investor. The investor directly owns all assets held in the account. Also called "separate account."

Sharpe Ratio: a risk-adjusted measure of portfolio performance in which risk is measured by the standard deviation of the portfolio's returns. Mathematically, over an evaluation period, it is the annualized ratio of excess return (actual return less the risk-free return) of the portfolio divided by the portfolio's standard deviation.

Staff: the professionals who, on a day-to-day basis, administer the investment program of a fund.

Standard Deviation: a statistical measure of the variability (range of potential outcomes) of investment returns.

Stock: see Common Stock.

Stress Test: a form of analysis in which one estimates the impact of various adverse situations on the returns of a portfolio.

Taft–Hartley fund: a multi-employer defined-benefit plan whose beneficiaries are members of a labor union with members working for multiple employers.

Time-Weighted Rate of Return: the rate of return on a portfolio over a particular period of time. Effectively, it is the return on $1.00 invested in the portfolio at the beginning of the measurement period.

Trustee: a person who has fiduciary responsibility for a pool of assets.

Uncertainty: the state of incomplete knowledge about the present and future with respect to an investment.

Uncorrelated: condition in which the returns of two or more assets do not go in the same direction at the same time.

Underfunded: the status of a fund whose assets are less in value than the liabilities for which those assets exist.

Value Stocks: a segment of an equity market characterized by the stocks of companies that have experienced poor past price performance or whose issuing companies have experienced relatively poor past earnings compared with the market as a whole. They tend to display low price-to-earnings ratios relative to the market. Also called "distressed stocks."

Venture Capital: a form of private equity involving non-publicly traded equity investments in which a general partner provides capital to an entrepreneur to begin or grow an enterprise with the intention of eventually making a profit by taking the company public or selling it to another business.

Volatility: the characteristic that financial asset returns vary over time in unpredictable ways or amounts. This term is often used interchangeably with the standard deviation of the asset's returns.

Further Reading

Legal Basics

The basic legal principles of fiduciary responsibility are found in this material (but you will still need a lawyer):

> National Conference of Commissioners of Uniform State Laws. 1994. "Uniform Prudent Investors Act" (www.law.upenn.edu/bll/archives/ulc/fnact99/1990s/upia94.pdf).

Must-Reads

Three top-notch general interest books on investing that provide a basic education in sound investment principles are as follows (start with Malkiel):

> Bernstein, Peter L. 1996. *Against the Gods: The Remarkable Story of Risk.* New York: John Wiley & Sons.

> Chancellor, Edward. 2000. *Devil Take the Hindmost: A History of Financial Speculation.* New York: Plume.

> Malkiel, Burton G. 2007. *A Random Walk Down Wall Street: The Time-Tested Strategy for Successful Investing.* Revised and updated ed. New York: W.W. Norton.

Further Education

Following are seven well-written, highly regarded books about investing. Swensen's book, in particular, deals with setting up a superior investment management process (actual investment results, of course, are not guaranteed):

> Bernstein, Peter L. 2005. *Capital Ideas: The Improbable Origins of Modern Wall Street.* New York: John Wiley & Sons.

> Bogle, John C. 2010. *Common Sense on Mutual Funds.* Fully updated 10th anniversary ed. Hoboken, NJ: John Wiley & Sons.

> Bookstaber, Richard. 2007. *A Demon of Our Own Design: Markets, Hedge Funds, and the Perils of Financial Innovation.* Hoboken, NJ: John Wiley & Sons.

Ferguson, Niall. 2008. *The Ascent of Money: A Financial History of the World.* New York: Penguin Press.

Graham, Benjamin. 2003. *The Intelligent Investor.* Revised ed. Updated with new commentary by Jason Zweig. New York: HarperCollins Publishers, HarperBusiness Essentials.

Montier, James. 2010. *The Little Book of Behavioral Investing: How Not to Be Your Own Worst Enemy.* Hoboken, NJ: John Wiley & Sons.

Swensen, David F. 2000. *Pioneering Portfolio Management: An Unconventional Approach to Institutional Investment.* New York: Simon & Schuster, Free Press.

Ethical and Professional Standards

The first two publications deal with standards for investment managers and staff; the other three cover standards for trustees:

CFA Institute. 2010. *Code of Ethics and Standards of Professional Conduct.* Charlottesville, VA: CFA Institute (www.cfapubs.org/doi/pdf/10.2469/ccb.v2010.n14.1).

Schacht, Kurt, Jonathan J. Stokes, and Glenn Doggett. 2009. *Asset Manager Code of Professional Conduct.* 2nd ed. Charlottesville, VA: CFA Institute (www.cfapubs.org/toc/ccb/2009/2009/8).

Schacht, Kurt, Jonathan J. Stokes, and Glenn Doggett. 2010. *Investment Management Code of Conduct for Endowments, Foundations, and Charitable Organizations.* Charlottesville, VA: CFA Institute (www.cfapubs.org/toc/ccb/2010/2010/15).

CFA Institute. 2008. *Code of Conduct for Members of a Pension Scheme Governing Body.* Charlottesville, VA: CFA Institute (www.cfapubs.org/doi/abs/10.2469/ccb.v2008.n3.1).

Stanford Program in Law, Economics, & Business. 2007. "Best Practice Principles." Stanford Institutional Investors' Forum, Committee on Fund Governance (www.law.stanford.edu/program/executive/programs/Clapman_Report-070316v6-Color.pdf).

©2011 The Research Foundation of CFA Institute

Textbooks and Articles

This small volume expands on many of the topics in Sessions 4, 6, and 7 and provides trustees a non-quantitative discussion of evaluating investment performance:

> Siegel, Laurence B. 2003. *Benchmarks and Investment Management.* Charlottesville, VA: Research Foundation of the CFA Institute.

A useful discussion of performance evaluation is also presented in this chapter:

> Bailey, Jeffery V., Thomas M. Richards, and David E. Tierney. 2009. "Evaluating Portfolio Performance." In Investment Performance Measurement. 1st ed. Edited by Philip Lawton and Todd Jankowski. Charlottesville, VA: CFA Institute:11–78.

For those trustees with the time and interest, this textbook sponsored by CFA Institute provides comprehensive and in-depth—but largely nontechnical—coverage of all aspects of institutional investing:

> Maginn, John L., Donald L. Tuttle, Dennis W. McLeavey, and Jerald E. Pinto. 2007. *Managing Investment Portfolios: A Dynamic Process.* 3rd ed. Hoboken, NJ: John Wiley & Sons.

The one journal article we recommend is by a Nobel-Prize-winning economist and comes to a startling conclusion that should keep all of us humble:

> Sharpe, William F. 1991. "The Arithmetic of Active Management." Financial Analysts Journal, vol. 47, no. 1 (January/February):7–9.

Made in the USA
Charleston, SC
15 April 2011

Named Endowments

The Research Foundation of CFA Institute acknowledges with sincere gratitude the generous contributions of the Named Endowment participants listed below.

Gifts of at least US$100,000 qualify donors for membership in the Named Endowment category, which recognizes in perpetuity the commitment toward unbiased, practitioner-oriented, relevant research that these firms and individuals have expressed through their generous support of the Research Foundation of CFA Institute.

Ameritech
Anonymous
Robert D. Arnott
Theodore R. Aronson, CFA
Asahi Mutual Life
Batterymarch Financial Management
Boston Company
Boston Partners Asset Management, L.P.
Gary P. Brinson, CFA
Brinson Partners, Inc.
Capital Group International, Inc.
Concord Capital Management
Dai-Ichi Life Company
Daiwa Securities
Mr. and Mrs. Jeffrey J. Diermeier
Gifford Fong Associates
John A. Gunn, CFA
Jon L. Hagler Foundation
Investment Counsel Association
   of America, Inc.
Jacobs Levy Equity Management
Long-Term Credit Bank of Japan, Ltd.
Lynch, Jones & Ryan

Meiji Mutual Life Insurance Company
Miller Anderson & Sherrerd, LLP
John B. Neff, CFA
Nikko Securities Co., Ltd
Nippon Life Insurance Company of Japan
Nomura Securities Co., Ltd.
Payden & Rygel
Provident National Bank
Frank K. Reilly, CFA
Salomon Brothers
Sassoon Holdings Pte Ltd.
Scudder Stevens & Clark
Security Analysts Association of Japan
Shaw Data Securities, Inc.
Sit Investment Associates, Inc.
Standish, Ayer & Wood, Inc.
State Farm Insurance Companies
Sumitomo Life America, Inc.
T. Rowe Price Associates, Inc.
Templeton Investment Counsel Inc.
Travelers Insurance Co.
USF&G Companies
Yamaichi Securities Co., Ltd.

Senior Research Fellows

Financial Services Analyst Association

For more on upcoming Research Foundation
publications and webcasts, please visit
www.cfainstitute.org/foundation/products/index.html.

Research Foundation monographs
are online at www.cfapubs.org.